Managing Without the CEO

Managing Without the CEO

Jack Asgar
Richard Wigley

Universal Publishers
USA • 2000

Managing Without the CEO

Copyright © 2000 Jack Asgar & Richard Wigley
All rights reserved.

ISBN: 1-58112-711-1

Universal Publishers
USA • 2000

www.upublish.com/books/asgar.htm

DEDICATION

We dedicate this book to our former partner and mentor Frank O. Hoffman. Without Frank this book could not have been written. His lifetime work in the field of management and organizational training has been a guiding light to us as well as the clients of Practical Management, Inc. Unfortunately Frank was too busy guiding others to write a book. Had he published his work, every reader would have known that he was at least twenty years ahead of his time.

We are grateful for his teachings and consider ourselves blessed to have known him in our professional careers.

TABLE OF CONTENTS

DEDICATION .... *v*

INTRODUCTION .... *ix*

UNITY *13*

THE OBSTACLES TO GREATNESS *21*

THE HIERARCHY *37*

THE MISSION WORKER *58*

SUPERVISORS: MANAGEMENT'S TECHNICAL EXPERTS ... *82*

MANAGING A MULTI-LEVEL ORGANIZATION *100*

THE POWER BROKERS *149*

TOP EXECUTIVES: EXTERNAL MANAGEMENT *170*

INTRODUCTION

In this book you will find a unique and multi-dimensional view of managing that has been missing in almost all of the popular management books. MANAGING WITHOUT THE CEO is a guide to creating a business management system that fosters a supportive, successful relationship between the four basic segments of the business equation: the employees, the investors or stockholders, the customers, and the community in which the employees live and the business functions. Despite recent trends to the contrary, it is clear that the health of each of these four segments is crucial to keeping the whole unit in balance. The driving theme of this book is managing for equilibrium between these parts, striking a balance in serving each segment's needs. We believe this equilibrium can best be achieved by developing and maintaining a hierarchical system of knowledge and management that enables all levels within any company to perform at optimum effectiveness.

Unfortunately, current trends in management have created major threats to the equilibrium of business. The threats come primarily from some of the CEOs of major companies. These new CEOs have come from the field of finance or marketing, neither of which adequately prepares CEOs for managing an organization.

One result of this trend is that too much emphasis has been paid in recent years to shareholder success (profit) at the expense of the overall health of a company, its employees, the customers it serves, and the community in which it exists. This trend has had disastrous results for U.S. workers and customers. It has moved countless jobs out of local communities and into foreign countries where pay is low and conditions are far below our standards.

This short-sighted, short-term focus has resulted in the ascension of CEOs such as Albert "Chainsaw" Dunlap, who was hired at an astronomical price for the express purpose of cutting the number of employees at companies to improve shareholders' earning in the short run. This kind of CEO is often in and out before he has to face the consequences of his or her actions. While the employees are the most directly effected by firings, lay-offs, and out-sourcing, customer service often suffers in the bargain, too. Recent studies show that customer satisfaction with service is very low in industries across the board. And it's a truism that the disappearance of a major employer from a community can have devastating and far-reaching effects on that community.

These CEOs are taking their companies toward organizational suicide while filling their own pockets with the monies obtained from the toil of the workers, supervisors, middle managers, and the community.

In working with organizations of all types and sizes, we have developed an approach that helps create a business structure that fosters and provides equilibrium.

Equilibrium within a business requires discrete knowledge at each level of the organization. This knowledge(s) are neither housed in a single source, nor can it be spread among the employees haphazardly. Moreover, the knowledge(s) is not transferable from one level in the organization to the next. A hierarchy is needed to make sure that all knowledge(s) related to internal and external management of the business is available in the right place at the right time. We call this concept "the hierarchy of knowledge." In this hierarchy we identify the knowledge(s) and skills required at each level in order to assure total management performance. This approach avoids duplication of efforts and eliminates the need for additional layers of management, even in large companies. Additionally, this approach makes it possible for each member of the organization to make his or her optimum contribution. It defines individual accountability with precision, a factor that has been lacking in every "new" management approach used in the last fifteen years.

We have entitled this book MANAGING WITHOUT THE CEO, not because we don't respect the difficult job a CEO must perform, but because true internal organizational management must be performed by middle management and not by the CEO. The CEO, along with other top executives, should manage the critical external issues. This means he or she should be spending energy with major clients, dealing with government regulations, managing investor and financial relations, and devoting him or herself to entrepreneurship.

This book is all about how to make the concept of the hierarchy of knowledge apply in the organization and accomplish the business's mission successfully, meaning with least cost, fewer levels of management, and with great human dignity. All the bureaucracy in a typical management hierarchy can be eliminated once an organization understands and implements the concept of the hierarchy of knowledge rather than the hierarchy of the pecking order.

Our work and observations are not academic. They are built on our experience with real organizations, real people, and real issues. However, in authoring this book and in our work we have been influenced by the writing of Peter Drucker, who has observed organizations for decades and has been able to articulate the major issues very clearly. We have also been influenced by our former partner, Frank O. Hoffman, who formulated a practical approach to management —an approach that has been validated time and time again regardless of the changes in trends in business practices.

Our book also elucidates the knowledge necessary to achieve and manage a knowledge-based organization. Our concept of the hierarchy of knowledge provides the tools of productivity through the appropriate use of knowledge. Furthermore, it shows the way to a total organizational system for obtaining an effective "equilibrium" in managing employees, shareholders, customers, and the community.

We have tried in these pages to provide a multifaceted approach to managing which clearly identifies the hierarchies and provide a blueprint for comprehensive actions to be taken by each level of the hierarchy.

It appears that management thinking has come full circle. The one-dimensional mentality has run its course as organizations begin to find that without an organized system of management, customer service, re-engineering, teamwork, and quality initiatives will be only marginally successful.

CHAPTER ONE

UNITY

Marshalling the immense energy, vitality, and resources of the American people must become the driving force behind the return of this country to its former deserved status as the "greatest nation on earth." Given that our social and political institutions appear unable to meet this challenge, we must begin to recognize the enormous potential that the world of work offers for the revitalization of the American dream. Business and service organizations are in a unique position to provide the environment in which unity of people and purpose can be accomplished.

Where else is there greater opportunity for the greatest number of people to be recognized for their individual talents and skills? Where else is there opportunity for the greatest number of people to gain gratification and self-respect through accomplishment? What other institution or social entity provides the unique potential for individual performance as well as team contribution? For developing socialization skills, lasting relationships, and a sense of community? Business and service organizations can be the "great equalizers" in which people can grow and develop, regardless of ethnic background, religion, political orientation, education, nationality, race, sex, and age.

For many people work is a truly meaningful activity for reasons beyond economic necessity. Arlie Hochschild, director of the Center for Working Families at the University of California, Berkeley says, "When you ask people where they really feel appreciated, it's at work." Partially because of the failure of our other institutions and increased financial pressures, work has taken on a new and more meaningful status in today's world. Professor Lee Bolman from the University of Missouri in Kansas City maintains, "Work has become a predominant feature in everyday life. People want work to mean something. They are looking for shared beliefs." Fulfillment and gratification have risen to a level equal to, or greater than, economic benefits.

The words "potential" and "opportunities" have been used purposely in the preceding discussion of business and service organizations to show the unifying forces they can provide in today's environment. Fulfilling the potential and providing the opportunities are at the discretion of each of the business entities. Current economic pressures, increasing global competition, changing technology, and the information revolution are real pressures to which organizations must respond and which affect their ability to perform to their social capabilities.

Companies facing survival pressures, real or perceived, have in recent years abdicated their responsibilities to employees, their community, and society in general. Some organizations have indeed abused customer trust, cheated investors, and exploited workers after exporting jobs to other countries.

The New York Times (May 13, 1998) reported that: "Nike and other U.S. companies pay workers in China and Vietnam less than $2 a day and workers in Indonesia less than $1 a day." Nike and others that have followed Nike's lead defend their position by piously asserting that they have contributed to the economy of those countries through the creation of jobs. Mark L. Clifford in his commentary in Business Week (December 23, 1996) understood this problem very clearly. He wrote, "Too few executives understand that the clamor for ethical sourcing isn't going to disappear with the wave of a magic press release." Mr. Clifford reported that one Nike manager told him that, in many foreign countries, "If you don't have a job, you're a prostitute, a beggar, a thief." Such statements are as ludicrous as they are outrageous and are particularly galling in view of Nike's willingness to pay $2 a day to make the shoes while paying sports figures such as Michael Jordan over $40 million to advertise them.

Since Robert Owen, the Welsh philanthropist, began to show respect and dignity to his factory workers in early nineteenth-century England, managing has become, and continues to be, a people business. Because Owen knew that his workers were critical to the success of his factory, he implemented better working conditions and raised the minimum age for child labor. He also reduced work hours and provided meals for his workers. Although these issues may not be too significant today, in his time they were revolutionary.

Unfortunately, other forms of management malpractice of the nineteenth century are still with us, as reflected in the labor practices of companies such as Nike in their Asian plants. It is ironic that at the end of the twentieth century Mr. Philip Knight, Nike's chairman and CEO, has finally agreed to increase the minimum age for hiring new workers in shoe factories to eighteen. He is now catching up with early nineteenth-century England! It has taken almost two years from the time reporters started to write about the low pay and miserable working conditions in factories operated by companies such as Nike, Walt Disney Co., and Kathie Lee Gifford for their CEOs to respond. Policies of Nike and others of the same ilk are so distasteful that even Mr. Knight admits, "I truly believe that the American consumer does not want to buy products made in abusive conditions." (From Mr. Knight's speech at the National Press Club-May 12, 1998.)

The current business environment has produced conditions never before faced by business organizations. Reorganizations, mergers, massive downsizing, and the ever-increasing influence of investors have significantly altered the landscape of American companies. Millions of jobs have been lost while millions more, requiring different knowledge and skill sets, have been created. Long-term employees are let go, taking years of accumulated knowledge with them, only to be replaced by lower-paid youngsters, fresh out of school. Teenagers are supervising teenagers; recent MBA graduates are leading work groups made up of employees twice their age and with many times their experience.

Amidst the confusion of the current environment, companies continue to try to mix the old practices with the new. While sometimes misdirected, enormous resources continue to be devoted to increasing productivity, customer service, and quality-doing work the old fashioned way. The end results have often been successful in the short term, but disastrous in the long term when employees discover that downsizing often follows. Ironically, the people downsized are often those who contributed to the improvements. Rather than the reward for good work being better work and security, the reward of good work has become no work. Little wonder that employees resist improvement efforts, openly scoff at the concept of company loyalty, and revert to a job preservation mentality. Abraham Maslow's concept of the "Hierarchy of Needs" is more alive and well than ever.

At the organizational level, reorganizations and downsizing appear to be counterproductive. There is evidence from 1988 to 1994 to indicate that investor values in growing companies have outpaced the value of downsized companies (USA Today, 7, Feb., 1996.). Little wonder that Dwight Getz says, "Growth, not downsizing, leads to greatness." It has become increasingly clear that organizations cannot shrink to greatness. In fact, downsizing is backfiring in many companies. Business magazines such as Business Week and newspapers such as USA Today report that organizations that have downsized for profit are now being pushed by their competitors who gladly hire these experienced employees. At the same time, these competitors are winning away many of the customers of the downsized firms. The new term for this unusual phenomenon is "corporate judo," referring to the strategy of using an opponent's force and weight against him.

Glendale Federal benefited this way from the merger of Wells Fargo and First Interstate that resulted in seven thousand jobs disappearing. MCI took advantage in the same fashion after AT&T's announcement that forty thousand employees would have to be laid off.

Interfering with the basics has caused some of these misuses, such as when organizations have been viewed as a moneymaking vehicle for the investors only, without any obligation to the rest of the "stakeholders." The approach to management presented in succeeding chapters of this book, while offering no guarantees against top management transgressions or organizational upheaval provides an effective process for guiding organizations in their efforts to meet their goals and fulfill their responsibilities to employees. When a business follows certain fundamental concepts and practices, the organizational structure will almost always provide a stable environment in which abuses are rare and identified early.

Fundamental to the process of "managing without a CEO" is that organizations have moral, ethical, fiscal, and legal responsibilities to four major stakeholders: investors, employees, customers, and the community. In governmental organizations, investors are the taxpayers. Since all four components are analogous to the legs of a table, each is equally important if the table is to stand. Too much or too little emphasis on any stakeholder invariably has a detrimental effect on the others. Catering excessively to investors, which is the current trend, often leads to cost cutting and downsizing, even though the company is making a healthy profit. The negative impact on employees and the community is obvious. Not only do those laid off suffer the consequences but also those who remain often have to pick up the slack, working excessive hours with an increased job load and without any increase in compensation. Work overload and burnout have in recent years risen to the top of the list of employee concerns.

The tendency of organizations to value technology, investors, and profits considerably higher than they value their employees is seriously affecting the loyalty and dedication of employees. There is an undercurrent of unrest and insecurity among all of the stakeholders-except the investors. Employees and customers have become more assertive in expressing their dissatisfaction, and at times, hostility to employers. Loyalty and dedication are becoming attributes of the past.

And yet many companies seem to forget that the effects of customer and employee dissatisfaction on the profitability and the survival of companies are potentially devastating. Frederick F. Reishheld, in his important book, *The Loyalty Effect—The Hidden Faces Behind Growth, Profits, and Lasting Values*, contends that organizations need to be more than profit machines. Reishheld asserts that by maintaining a positive environment for loyal employees, companies can achieve "prodigious growth in profits and cash generation." Under Reishheld's management model, profit is the result of "value creation" and not the sole purpose of the company.

The economic good times of the '90s have enhanced the lives of many, particularly investors and stockholders. However, the price paid by millions of employees at all organizational levels has been enormous. In September 1997, slightly more than 7.8 million workers, representing 6 percent of the workforce, had two jobs according to the Bureau of Labor Statistics. Juggling two jobs, while providing short-term economic benefits, often has long-term negative effects. Burnout and stress, less time with spouses and children, and increased costs for such necessities as childcare, transportation, and clothes often defeat the purpose of having two jobs.

Beyond the economic effects, mergers, reorganizations, and downsizing have exacted a price in terms of basic human needs. Self-respect, personal fulfillment, gratification, social interaction, family security and stability-all enhanced by a stable work environment-have seriously eroded. Whether these are acceptable casualties in the march toward adapting to the New World of technology and globalization, as many economists and business leaders suggest, is a matter of debate.

Inevitably, the frenzy of mergers, reorganizations, and downsizing will come to an end-or at least slow to a manageable trickle-and a semblance of order will be restored. With the economic good times predicted to continue, the time is right for organizations to begin to assess and repair the damage that has been done to their stakeholders, particularly their employees, their customers, and the community.

Restoring order from chaos is never easy. But it starts by first creating a work environment that has structure and predictability, one in which expectations are clear and accountabilities are established. It starts by creating an environment in which all employees at all levels know what to do, how to do it, when to do it, and why. It starts with creating a work environment in which the consequences of good work and of poor work are clearly defined and carried out. In short, it starts when good management, particularly by supervisors and managers, is defined, demanded, and implemented. We believe a hierarchical system of management is the optimum system for accomplishing these worthy goals.

A structured organizational environment, like that provided by a well-managed hierarchy is a basic requirement for giving back to all employees that which has been lost in the current corporate environment. It gives back not only the opportunity to fulfill the basic human needs-of self-support and sufficiency-but allows employees to regain the self-respect, gratification, fulfillment, and sense of community so sadly lacking in today's business environment.

Business organizations would be well served by looking back in order to move forward. The basic concepts presented in this book are good places to start. It has taken only a few decades to seriously erode the value that business organizations had once provided to society as a whole.

Reversing that course must occur soon if business organizations are going to fulfill their mandate to provide a cohesive entity in which people can help establish themselves as productive adults, and support themselves and their families.

CHAPTER TWO

THE OBSTACLES TO GREATNESS

Up until this century, business and commerce have not been held in high esteem by those in the middle to high levels of the social-political-intellectual strata of society. Moneychangers, shop owners, tradespeople, and service people were variously considered charlatans, money-grubbers, or simply disparaged as hired help. At times, in many cultures, foreign workers were imported to do the menial tasks considered well below the dignity of the native population to perform. Generation after generation often continued in this same menial position, having little opportunity to better their station in life.

In the New World, after the Industrial Revolution and well into the twentieth century, the status of business took on greater legitimacy and being employed as a businessperson became a position of higher social standing. In the 1950s, humanity and community became more important to a developing Corporate America. "People are our greatest asset" was not just a platitude, but also a reality in the policies and practices of the forward-thinking decision-makers. Reward systems, pay for performance, and a host of other "bennies" became symbolic of a company's respect for its employees and their well being. Employees repaid their employers with hard work, inventiveness, and a sense of loyalty. People were proud to say what they did and for whom they worked.

How things have changed in the last decade. Many U.S. corporations, including some of the larger, more respected Fortune 500 companies, have precipitously turned the tables on the people who helped them achieve their success. Loyalty is no longer a virtue in the face of massive downsizing that seems to come with little or no warning. While the effects on the ranks of the now unemployed or the soon-to-be unemployed is disastrous, the effects on the larger body politic is likely to be catastrophic as well. Corporate America is in a unique position to offer the security, the sense of identity and community, and the social infrastructure once provided by our other failing social institutions. If it does not take advantage of that unique position, it is not too great a stretch to say that society at large will suffer for it.

The rash of current books, articles, editorials, and news commentaries lamenting businesses' abdication of its social and moral responsibilities is solid evidence that this is a severe national problem. The federal government was considering legislation to force companies to become more "responsible." While this is certainly not a solution, it attests to the severity of the problem.

Is all hope gone? Is there still time to redeem the social and moral commitments that all organizations should have to the hands that feed them? Yes. But only if we have the fortitude and the courage to deal with the forces that are driving the downward spiral. In many instances it's the denizens of the executive suites who are running roughshod over the values and virtues that made the U.S. the leader of the business world. While attaining enormous personal wealth and power, they are slowly but surely undermining the social, communal, and personal values that employees have the right to expect from companies to which they devote their lives.

Fortunately there are CEOs such as Aaron Feuerstein who refused to lay off his employees after a fire closed his Malden Mills. He even issued bonuses he had promised his people before the fire. Or, Kenneth A. Lehman and David A. Weinberg, Co-Chairmen of Feel-Pro, who have followed innovative human resource practices that have fostered teamwork and unusually low employee turnover. The company has grown at the rate of 18 percent since 1992, with a 40 percent margin above industry norms. Even in selling the company to Federated-Mogul Corporation, they made sure to negotiate to keep the unique company culture intact.

While many businesses and their leadership continue to retain the values and virtues that made this country a leader in the global business world, others seem bent on destroying that fabric in the name of progress, technology, and global competition. And they're all getting rave reviews from Wall Street, their investors, and the business media. When the unemployment figures for February 1996 were better than expected, the stock market took it's third biggest nose-dive in history. This led one newscaster to quip, "What's good for Main Street is not good for Wall Street." Like the forces that drove the lowly status of business centuries ago, the current ones also sit at the top of the social food chain-in executive suites, boardrooms, investment houses, in company jets, in mansions on wholly owned islands, and on an unconscionable pile of stock options.

These false prophets of industry fall into three categories.

THE GREED MONGERS

People who work hard and make significant contributions to their organizations deserve to be paid well, at whatever level the work is performed. Equal pay for equal performance, equity and fairness, equitable ratios of salary between management levels, profit sharing, and team rewards are all topics that have dominated the current Human Resources literature and the compensation policies. Commendable to be sure.

But in reality its just more smoke being blown up the collective noses of employees and lower-level management. It takes resources and a willingness to sacrifice other financial goals in favor of a few more bucks in the paychecks of deserving personnel. In the face of downsizing, re-engineering, out-sourcing, technology upgrades, and increased investor dividends, workers hear, "the money simply isn't there, folks. Maybe next year. But, by the way, I need all of you to work extra hard and extra hours to make up for our recent layoffs." Just read this newspaper announcement, "Xerox Corporation Chairman and Chief Executive, Paul A. Allaire, made $7.5 million in salary and bonuses in 1997, up from $4.0 million in 1996...The disclosure follows Xerox's announcement that it will cut 9,000 jobs, or about 10 percent of its work force of 91,400."

With the stock market having its best years, many companies making huge profits and economic indicators on the rise, where is all of the money going? For one, into the pockets of those who sit at the top of the heap. Salaries, pay raises, and overall compensation of executives and CEOs have skyrocketed to the extent that one tick on the Stock Market moves literally millions of dollars in personal wealth. In the 1970s, the ratio of average pay for large company CEOs to their employees was 41 to 1; in 1992 the ratio had increased to 145 to 1; in 1994, the ratio was 187 to 1; in 1996, 326 to 1 (USA Today); in 1998 it had reached 419 to 1, and is still increasing (Institute for Policy Studies & United for Fair Economy.) Had the pay increases for average workers grown at the same rate as for the CEOs, a factory worker today would receive $110,400 a year instead of $29,270.

The existence of quadruple-digit compensation for any single individual in companies that are doing well is at best unfair to the employees who see little monetary benefit. In organizations that are not doing well-some in Chapter 11 bankruptcy, some on the verge of buy-out, or laying off thousands of employees-such compensation is unconscionable, if not immoral. In the health care industry where a near state of national emergency exists in terms of costs, quality of service, and facilities, CEOs receive 35 percent higher compensation than those in companies of similar size. (USA Today, Feb. 20, 1996). Pay for performance, indeed!

In a recent newscast, a prominent business correspondent attempted to respond to the greed factor involving company executives by explaining that much of their wealth is on paper and not in their pockets. Tell that to the next CEO candidate to be offered a take-over position in your company and see how quickly he or she heads for the door. The greed mongers feed on stock options, on occasion accepting lower salaries in favor of a bigger chunk of potential ownership. Why? Because it it's a good deal for the company since it's not an out-of-pocket cost, and if the stock goes up, that's good for everybody (but only tangentially for the employees). It's also an enormous benefit to the new CEO because of the established price and the potential gains with stock increases. And because they can't lose. Wall Street doesn't really care about the long-term health of a company; investors want their profits immediately; stock prices are in the here and now. On the day that AT&T announced a lay-off of 40,000 employees, their stock increased several points, increasing not only the wealth of AT&T executives but making them the darlings of their investors.

Any CEO looking to fill his or her pockets need look only for the quickest and fastest way to nudge the ticker. Cost cuts, downsizing, re-engineering, sell-offs, plant shut downs, salary freezes-any or all can produce short-term gains, stock value increases, and millions of dollars for the quick-buck artists of mahogany row. These options have been known to run into the hundreds of millions, one as high as $200 million. No CEO is worth that much money no matter how much that CEO has contributed to the organization.

In the early 1990s, AT&T purchased NCR for more than $7 billion, a very high price according to at least one financial expert. Prior to the purchase, NCR was doing well under the leadership of Charles Exley, who had awakened this sleeping giant after several years of less than peak performance. AT&T's logic was to increase the value and performance of it's computer division, which was not doing well at all. In the process, stock options were exercised and several AT&T executives increased their personal worth several fold. Once the transition was complete, AT&T proceeded to fire the NCR executives who were very successful under Mr. Exley, and replace them with their own executives who had not been able run to their own computer division. Of course the takeover was a dismal failure-except to those who added significantly to their net worth from stock options.

Executives in most companies are well protected financially regardless of the performance of their organizations. On record are bonuses, salary increases, and stock options paid to executives of companies whose value and performance are, and often have been, declining for years. Even when they're fired-finally-they leave with "golden parachutes" or "poison pills," while others in the organization may not have received anything but a pink slip and an application for unemployment. Certainly the joke is on us, the joke being "pay for performance," "equal pay for equal work," and all that other malarkey that executives sign their names to with no intention of applying them to anyone but themselves.

Unfortunately there are many examples of such greed mongers. Lawrence Tisch, the CEO of CBS made out with $900 million in ten years—and was called a hero on Wall Street. However, those ten years were wrapped in cost cutting and downsizing. Walter Cronkite has said of Tisch's tenure "Some discipline in spending was necessary. But what happened, it got way past fat and then to flesh and to muscle and then to amputation." It is a sad situation when the "amputation" of others produces $900 million for the CEO.

Stephen Wiggins, the founder and former Chairman of Oxford Health Plans, Inc., despite leaving the company in turmoil, received $9 million and "assorted benefits" in severance pay. No need to ask what kind of severance compensation the regular employees received.

In these days of white-collar crime, the actions of the greed mongers should warrant felony charges. How different are they from thieves of any other ilk? Their credo is basically the same: take other people's money and run, without a single glance back at the destruction and devastation left behind. And where do they run? To another company to repeat the same crime all over again.

THE BEAN COUNTERS

Counted among the ranks of executive management is a particularly virulent strain of organism often referred to as "the money men." While the work they do is full of the complexities of statistics, forecasts, and price-earnings ratios, they fundamentally believe there are only two meaningful factors in organizational life: credits and debits. Credits are good; debits are bad; increase the former; decrease the latter.

While these bean counters may not be as avaricious as the greed mongers, and their goal may not be only to enrich themselves, the net results of their decisions are often just as devastating. To make major decisions solely by the numbers not only discounts human and social factors, but exemplifies the same short-sightedness that contributed to the nose dive that American business took in the 1970s and 1980s. We continue in the same arrogance that did not allow us to see the creeping incursion of foreign companies into major segments of our market place and overseas goods becoming the products of choice for our own consumers.

Between 1980 and 1990, best-selling authors and executives including C. Edwards Deming, Joseph M. Juran, Philip B. Crosby, and Tom Peters, came to the rescue riding their white horses into corporate boardrooms with heretical concepts such as customer service, product integrity and quality, process improvement, and empowerment. How quickly "total quality management" and "customer service" became the key watchwords in every major boardroom across the country, particularly in those companies in which the death rattle could be heard loud and clear. The real key to success? Total commitment from top management; a manifesto (otherwise known as a Mission Statement) signed in blood by all the executives, the greed mongers and bean counters among them. Finally, we were putting our money where our mouth is-people are our most important asset. Progress was being made (and still is in some companies), and people were once again excited about their jobs and the newfound respect they were given (and still enjoy in some companies). Product quality and good customer service were beginning to make us strongly competitive again. In general, things were looking up.

That was then; this is now. Enter the bean counters with the impatience indigenous to their species. In their minds, progress was simply too slow; we had fallen too far behind in the balance sheets. Survival depended upon more drastic action. To improve the appearance of the balance sheet, our most important asset-the one that had brought American business back to respectability- suddenly became our biggest liability. Bolstered by high-powered consultants and learned academicians anxious to make their fortune or tenure, bean counters have been in the forefront of the biggest morality crisis American business has faced in the Twentieth century. Jobs have migrated overseas; re-engineering has become a euphemism for replacing people with machines; mergers and acquisitions have made bigger profit centers within companies and have made smaller better. The net result? Better balance sheets for now. The costs? Hundreds of thousands of people laid off or displaced; plants, offices, and branches shut down; economies of local communities ruined; employees shedding all semblance of loyalty; and a crisis of confidence and trust in the integrity of business and business leaders.

Morality and humanity have taken a back seat to the balance sheet. Jobs that have been shipped overseas are now being performed in countries that do not have our laws governing safe or healthy working environments. Again American companies are profiting from "sweat shop" environments that would not be tolerated in this country and would be damned in outrage by the very companies that are promoting it in other countries. Talking out of both sides of the mouth is an inherent trait of the bean counter.

How often have we heard that "our labor costs are too high. American workers have priced themselves out of the market." Farm the jobs out, produce at lower costs, and improve profits so that re-engineering with high-tech equipment is possible. And, in the process, put American workers on the street.

Keith H. Hominids, in his commentary about protectionism, ("America's Hate Affair With Big Business; What Can Be Done About It?" Business Week: March 4, 1996) echoes many writers and commentators in the business media when he says, "Surely we can't bring back jobs in textiles and shoes. Low-skilled workers have to retool themselves for a high-skill economy..." Low-skilled workers have to retool themselves? Do we owe them nothing? Have they not earned the right to be retooled by the companies they caused to prosper? Our so-called high-skilled economy didn't just suddenly appear. It's been coming for several decades and yet it's only now that we're beginning to bemoan the lack of retooled employees. Such is the price we pay for tolerance-and more often reverence-of those in high places who live for today's stock prices and willfully disdain the requirements of tomorrow's reality. And the price, as usual, has to be paid by those in the retooling line.

Even if these employees are "retooled," how long will the bean counters put up with the much higher salary costs that will be required? How long will it take them to start looking for cheaper labor elsewhere? Hominids' strategy doesn't solve the problem, it only prolongs it. Until the residents of mahogany row begin to look beyond the balance sheet, the vicious cycle is destined to continue.

A further indication of the tendency toward double talk is the bean counter's pious pronouncement that "people are our most important asset." Not only does this represent a sop to the employees; it also takes hypocrisy to new heights. The last thing the bean counter considers people to be is an asset. Desks, equipment, inventory, buildings, land - they are the bean counter's assets. They hold a position of honor on the balance sheet and are to be coveted. People as assets? Certainly not to the bean counter. They're debits; they're liabilities; they're costs and overhead and fixed expenses, the biggest single dollar sign on everybody's budget. This mindset may be the fatal flaw that eventually topples the bean counters and the greed mongers and indeed may contribute to the massive upheaval that American business seems destined to suffer. At some point in the near future people will say "Enough!" Enough to being considered less valuable than a desk or a computer, and to being thrown out on the street as the most expedient way to make the annual report look good.

THE BELIEVERS OF "DEUS EX MACHINA"

Authors of Greek tragedies and some of today's CEOs may have something in common. They faced similar problems and came up with similar solutions. The dramatists often created story lines so complex and convoluted that there was no way that mere mortals could possibly resolve them. And, of course, audiences demanded resolution. The dramatists found a very convenient solution. In literary terms it is called deus ex machina. They had their gods appear on the stage via large cranes. Then the Gods could literally solve any problem, human or otherwise. Audiences could go away happy.

Many CEOs suffer from the deus ex machina syndrome. Faced with business tragedies, often self-inflicted, they invoke the supreme beings of business to apply their magic. They select from the current list of "deities" who sit perched on pedestals created from having written a book, conducted a study, designed a model, put a new spin on Business 101, or simply concocted a new mix of psycho-socio-anthro-babble. No matter how difficult or complex the problem, how elaborate and apparently beyond the abilities of mere mortals, the solutions may be, there is a consultant out there somewhere with a ready quick fix. And there are CEOs ready to spend the millions it will take for the invocation that will resolve the irresolvable. However complex the problem, the gods of American business can always reach for the New York Times best seller list and summon up the millions necessary to "revolutionize" the organization. And another fad is born.

The examples of fads that have arisen from the deus ex machina syndrome in American business are legendary for their notoriety and costs. The most prolific generation of fads has come from the application of psychological concepts and theories. So, from the social science that thrives on very intimate doctor-patient relationships comes the "one-size-fits-all" approach to organizational improvement, promoted by people who have never managed a business a day in their lives, and whose concerns were far removed from the realities of management.

Most pervasive of all was "Sensitivity Training" and all of its clones, offshoots, and subcultures. Popularized by Carl Rogers in the 1960s, Sensitivity Training was commercialized and marketed to organizations as a way for people to get in touch with themselves and to somehow parlay that self-realization into better performance on the job. Enormous sums of money were spent to send employees to retreats and ashrams, often to be abused and sometimes humiliated into becoming "sensitive." Many still bear the scars of those encounters.

"Quality Circles" were the next panacea applied by the CEOs. It is contemporary enough that some organizations still have a limited number of "circles" in operation. The original intent was to provide employees with an outlet to raise issues and voice concerns in a non-intimidating environment. In many instances, the primary players and expert consultants were the same ones (or their disciples) who led the charge in Sensitivity Training and other forms of social experimentation. The results, therefore, were the same: a seemingly good concept corrupted by the attempts of non-business people whose motives were most often not in concert with good business practices.

Close on the heels of the Quality Circles came C. Edwards Deming, and the "Japanese Experience." The rush was on to embrace the Team Concept, Total Quality Management (TQM), and its successor, re-engineering. Never before have so many CEOs signed such high-priced contracts with so many miracle workers.

While the basic concepts and principles of teams and TQM are not fads (Re-engineering being an exception), the methods of implementation touted by the self-proclaimed TQM gurus are inexorably moving in that direction. The fads in TQM are the implementation processes, which are again causing top management to lose sight of the fundamentals of managing an organization. It is but another in a long string of examples in which the believers of deus ex machina look to the theorists and quasi-experts to determine the course rather than referring to the fundamentals that have been the backbone of American business since its inception. Concepts and practices that are rooted in long-term successes and have staying power should not be abandoned simply because someone has written a book or advanced a new theory.

Perhaps the most degenerative use of the deus ex machina syndrome is the current trend toward throwing high technology-or any technology-at every conceivable problem an organization faces, Re-engineering being a classic case in point. After all, machines don't have to be managed, don't talk back, are never late to work, and don't ask for pay raises. What's more, they produce standard, predictable products at predictable costs. Add all that to the fact that machines are assets, and you have to ask, who in their right mind would not replace people with machines?

While there is no question of the value of machinery in organizations of all kinds, the complete story is not a pretty one. Talk to some of the agencies in the state governments of California, Nevada, and Oregon about the recent botched implementation of computer systems; talk to the Denver Airport Authority about it's high-tech baggage system; to auto companies who have thrown out parts of their computerized assembly processes and replaced them with people. And what happened to the age of the robots? These are expensive experiments that have all the trappings of foolish fads.

Even if we concede the benefits of today's high-tech mania, who receives those benefits and for what purposes? The employees? Again, they get the short end of the stick. Go ye forth and get retooled and maybe you can get a job somewhere else. Even if machines don't entirely replace employees, companies aren't too bashful about reminding employees of their value in relation to the machines they operate. A company that manufactures truck engines has machines throughout its plants with metal bands on which are printed the dollar value of the machine. None of the employees have similar value bands on their arms.

Managers and supervisors as beneficiaries? In terms of lay-offs and demotions, these groups are the biggest victims of the machine craze. Even when retained, they often become slaves to, or baby-sitters of, the new machine on the block. Didn't we conclude that the inhumanity and the depersonalization of work on the early Ford-style assembly line were detrimental to both employees and industry? We may be approaching that era again.

Are consumers ever benefactors? To a large degree, yes. Technology has provided tremendous benefits in both the public and the private sector. Getting cash at an ATM and using scanners at the supermarket make life somewhat easier, as does the efficiency of issuing airline tickets and hotel reservations by computer. It works as long as nothing goes wrong or the computer is not asked to do something out of the ordinary. But if it goes off for only a nanosecond, human beings may then have to deal with the transaction-or be available to suffer the wrath of antagonized customers. These are the same customers who, often, have had to navigate the maze of computerized telephone answering schemes seemingly put in place to frustrate even the most patient disgruntled customer. The public could tolerate even these bouts of consumer dissatisfaction if the promises of lower prices and better service through technology were ever fulfilled. But the frustration of consumers grows as the processes of business become less and less personal and more and more mechanized, as service people seem to be less accountable for customer satisfaction

Put aside the hype. Technology is ultimately for the benefit of the maker, not the user. When was the last time that savings from better inventory control, reduced personnel costs, and more efficient product distribution have been passed on to the consumer? On the other hand, passing the costs of new equipment and technology to the consumer is a foregone conclusion. You need look no further than your local bank for the reduced personal services, the increased dependence on technology, and the fee gouging that has accompanied the change. The credo appears to be: offer a free new service like ATM machines until the suckers get used to it, then charge them through the nose. And by the way, should they want to talk to a teller, we'll charge them for that as well. And we call this the age of customer service!

Top management's love affair with technology of any kind has also significantly changed the power structure within organizations. Today, business decisions are often based on what the machines can or cannot do; projects are planned around the capabilities and limitations of in-place technology; and Management Information Systems (MIS) departments are calling the shots. The cycle is endless and vicious. Having masterminded a dependency on technology, computer companies, MIS executives, and CEOs have established a survival strategy for themselves that guarantees not only lifetime security, but also untold wealth and power derived from planned obsolescence and built-in short-term machine limitations. Surely there are people in the technology business who knew that the year 2000 was coming and that existing computer technology should have been designed to accommodate this change. Yet the costs with changing those crucial four digits ran into the billions.

Taking business out of the hands of human beings and placing it on a computer chip has been one of the most massive con jobs in recent history. It is hucksters sitting in the boardrooms of computer companies who devise the strategies to sell the hucksters sitting in the boardrooms of client companies the technology that could not deliver what it promised. It is a form of poetic justice that one huckster cons another. There would be some comfort in that if it were not for the price paid by the real victims - the real people doing real jobs whose reward is a pink slip.

It is indeed fortunate that these false prophets sitting in corporate boardroom are in the minority among CEOs. Far outnumbering those are company executives whose concerns, policies, and actions are driven by the need to maintain equilibrium among all those who have a stake in their employees. Rarely do you see them featured in the dominant business journals. Their companies may not be major contributors to the GNP nor the darlings of the investment community. They are the solid citizens of the business world, respected, if not revered, by their employees, their investors, and their customers. They often serve on the boards of local public and private organizations and contribute generously to civic and charitable causes. If business is going to fulfill its promise as the institution that brings this country to its senses, the CEOs who champion the causes of all their constituents are the ones most likely to lead the way.

CHAPTER THREE

THE HIERARCHY

In today's chaotic business environment, organizational structure is once again under attack. Arising from the ashes of the quality crisis of the 1980s and 1990s is a concerted effort to declare the demise of the traditional organizational structure-the hierarchy. In their effort to capitalize on the "sorry state of American business," consultants and management theorists, many of whom have never managed anything, have taken dead aim at the hierarchy as the villain in this self-proclaimed war.

These consultants and management theorists wish to create an entity that is contrary to the basic structure of an organization. Hierarchy exists in every organization. That is to say there is always a top executive group, there is middle management, there is first-line supervision, and finally there is a group which actually performs the day-to-day function of the unit. No one can deny the existence of these groups no matter what the groups are named and how they are shown on an organization chart. The question is how the organization wants to use this natural structure. It can be used as a pecking order, it can be used as a command and control function, or, as we suggest, it can be used as a complement to total management of the organization by providing unique skills and knowledge at each level. We call this concept the Hierarchy of Knowledge.

Unfortunately, management has been a soft touch for the pundits advocating change since executives have long had a love-hate relationship with organizational hierarchy. When business is good, the hierarchical structure is the only way to go; when business is not so good, the hierarchy is the first and most immediate target for change. It is certainly easier to blame and try to fix an organizational chart than it is to seek out and correct the real causes for hard times.

Jack Gordon, writing in Training Magazine, stated "If all is not well in your traditionally structured hierarchical organization, the reason is that there are inherent, irreparable flaws in hierarchical systems that have rendered them obsolete here in the Information Age. Hierarchies are dinosaurs-lumbering, unable to adapt to the pace of change, paralyzed by complexity, and doomed to die." He goes on to characterize this view as the "prevailing management wisdom of the day."

Gordon's comments represent the typical confusion that exists about the differences between hierarchy and bureaucracy. The common tendency is to use the terms synonymously. Understanding the differences between the two is the first step in recognizing the true value of the hierarchy as the best fundamental structure of an organization. Organizational hierarchy specifically defines accountability and separation of unique skills and knowledge(s). Bureaucracy contains too many layers of management; each is engrossed in red tape and paper work and none has any defined and unique accountability.

"The age of the hierarchy is over," states James R. Houghton, CEO of Corning, who went on to restructure Corning into what he called a "global network." To state rhetorically that the use of hierarchy is over does not make it go away. A careful look at the "global network" will undoubtedly uncover a hierarchical structure hidden among and within the teams and units that make up the network.

Robert G. Eccles and Nithin Nohria, with James D. Berkley in their excellent book, *Beyond the Hype*, state: "For most people, this venerable organizational structure [the hierarchy] is considered bankrupt, seen as neither humane nor suitable for the demands imposed by a volatile and complex global economy. Exactly what will fill its shoes is a matter of some debate; scholars, consultants, and practitioners are all competing to define the contours of the new organization that will take the old one's place."

So what else is new? In the 1970s, scholars, consultants, and practitioners came out of the woodwork to spread the magic of matrix management, a somewhat complex structure popularized by the aerospace industry. In most common types of matrix management all functions work as one large conglomerate, divided into various projects headed by a project manager. Vestiges of both matrix management and project management still remain in some organizations, and rightfully so. But matrix management matured in the aerospace industry during the time when space exploration was at its height and comprehensive scientific experimentation into all types of technology was heavily funded. The need to gather and deploy resources of a highly specialized nature (in order to meet fine-tuned deadlines required by space exploration) created a structure that could apply those resources as demanded, project-by-project. Much of the success of the space program can be attributed to the flexibility of this structure, regardless of its complexity, its cost, and the difficulty in managing it.

True to their nature, hoards of scholars, consultants, and practitioners - flowcharts and models in hand - spread like locusts across corporate America selling the virtues of the matrix structure. It was clothed in the typical sociological garb of the management theorists. At this time, it was touted as the ultimate solution to the freedom-order, centralization-decentralization debate. As one might expect, many organizations fell in line, or fell for the line. Insurance companies, hospitals, government agencies, service organizations, and school systems became "matrixed," even though they shared very few of the organizational characteristics or operational objectives of the aerospace industry.

Matrix management and project management works when no one person can possibly have all of the appropriate technical knowledge to manage a unit. Aerospace companies were discovering new horizons unknown to mankind at the time. Insurance companies, schools, hospitals do not have the same mandate.

Other periodic challenges to hierarchies-functional, concentric, inverted, decentralized, and cluster structures-have come to life, made a brief splash in the literature, and disappeared. At Millipore (a global high-tech filtration company), an executive presented a tongue-in-cheek description of his approach to organizational structure. In a speech to the company's top fifty managers, he responded to the CEO's persistent emphasis on structural flexibility with a very wry definition of an ideal hybrid organizational structure. "Hybridization," he mused, "is an innovative, top-down, bottom-up, vertically-integrated organization, utilizing functionally focused groups and diversifying divisions, supporting each other in a soft matrix format, following the directives set forth by integrative devices called strategic business units." Double-talk aside, hybridization is simply one more example of the ambitious and complex management models designed to replace the simplicity and symmetry of a hierarchy.

Elliot Jaques, in his article "In Praise of Hierarchy," writes: "The managerial hierarchy is the most efficient, the hardest, and in fact, the most natural structure ever devised for large organizations." It is efficient because it defines how people are going to work in an organization. It is hard because at times it suffers from its simplicity and easiness. People often look for more complex issues. Because the technology in work has become complex does not mean that the structure by which the work gets done needs to be complex. As a matter of fact, the more complex the technology, the more simple an organizational structure one needs. Jaques goes on to say, "Properly structured, a hierarchy can release energy and creativity, rationalize productivity, and actually improve morale."

Hierarchy inherently defines and clarifies working relationships within an organization. It is the best and most practical structure to bring harmony and communication to the organization. However, hierarchy is not magic. It must be worked at constantly so that it does not evolve into bureaucracy.

Hierarchy gives the best chance of success and continuous improvement within a business structure. It must be redefined, however, within any given business to take into account the particular needs of some work units. For example, in a research unit the organization does not need the traditional hierarchy. The reason for this is that researchers tend to be more dedicated to their subject than they are dedicated to the company. They will seek research positions in any organization that offers a better research facility and more serious research. To try to change this basic axiom is counterproductive. Research units must be given a clear direction and then left alone to provide the best research they know how. The concept of self-management can work well in such units.

THE TEAM CHALLENGE

Teamwork-another prevailing management vision of the day-is the new heir apparent to the "old dinosaurs." Teamwork enthusiasts tout the "teamwork paradigm" as the logical counterpoint to the deficiencies of the hierarchical structure.

Interestingly enough, teaming by its nature is not antithetical to hierarchies, but all too often the methods of its implementation are. It is ironic that many of the people who advocate the demise of the hierarchy created the worst kinds of hierarchies in implementing the team concept. Those who think that the traditional hierarchy is plodding and cumbersome should witness the organizational chaos that occurs when committees become the power brokers. What such companies end up with are teams that report to quality committees that report to quality councils that report to an executive steering committee-all graphically represented by as many overlapping circles, arranged vertically, as there are committees.

Incredulously, these "committee hierarchies" were

meant to coexist with "operating hierarchies" in peaceful harmony. Total Quality Management (TQM) was to be the purview of the committees; keeping the organization running remained with the operating units. For those who advocate pure organizational chaos, this structure is a prototype. It's no mystery why the rush to dismantle hierarchies came so closely on the heels of the TQM movement.

When a team concept is created to supplement an existing operating hierarchy, or to provide a means to end-run it, failure and its associated costs are a foregone conclusion. When a team concept is embedded within the hierarchy (assuming the hierarchy is not a bureaucracy), it stands a very high chance of success. Natural work-group teams properly organized and managed, can often provide quality improvements, flexibility, and response to change. But they are still an integral part of a hierarchy. Supervision exists, although the role has changed to more support and direction and less control and decision-making. That's good supervision in any environment, with or without teams.

Autonomous work-groups, if they are to be successful, must also be an integral part of a hierarchy. Although supervision has been absorbed into the team and theoretically the position no longer exists, an informal hierarchy forms within the team, as it typically does with any group of people who work together for any length of time.

In addition, for autonomous teams to be successful over time, they must have a direct connection to the organization, most commonly to a manager within the organization. Obviously, this connection represents authority, a degree of veto power, and a source of resources and decision-making that is beyond the charter of the team. When that connection to the organization is insufficient, when the manager isn't functioning properly or isn't an adequate conduit for the team, the autonomous team is likely to fail. As much as the team likes its freedom at first, freedom means responsibility, and without proper support, freedom soon becomes a debilitating factor. Without an in-house managerial lifeline, the team will likely feel isolated by slow responses to resource requests and other decisions.

It's as true in the team concept as it is in any rational organizational structure that its effectiveness will be a direct function of how well it's managed. Poor management will cause any structure to fail; good management will cause it to flourish. It is axiomatic in a business environment that any organizational structure will work if the structure fits the nature of the business, and if people, particularly management, are willing and able to make it work.

In discussing the prevailing management wisdom of the day that favors a team environment and ridicules the hierarchical structure, Gerry Kraines, President and CEO of the Levinson Institute, refers to this prevailing wisdom as "the current state of mythology." He adds, "Mythology has gripped not just the American business world but also the business schools. It doesn't solve the problems. It only makes them worse. The problem is not with hierarchy, but with bad hierarchies."

Most of the criticisms of organizational hierarchy are about bad hierarchy. For example: "Managers make decisions in a vacuum without consulting those closest to the problem." (Jack Gordon, Training Magazine, August 1994.) We know of no hierarchical practice that suggests managers must make decisions without consulting with those closest to the problem. In a thriving hierarchical structure managers are accountable for the decisions they make.

There are other arguments against hierarchy that support our statement that many writers are using the terms "hierarchy" and "bureaucracy" synonymously. Mr. Gordon as a writer falls prey to this temptation and goes on to write, "Because bureaucracies value conformity, managers fall prey to groupthink." It is fascinating to listen to concepts espoused by the advocates of new age management. They preach that an effective leader must communicate his vision and get everyone on board with that vision; that teams must articulate their mission and all the members must buy into that mission. Apparently Gordon feels that is not groupthink. It is only groupthink when you achieve unanimity of agreement in a hierarchical format. Interesting double-talk.

Another critical point against hierarchy raised by Gordon is that "Managers waste endless hours in unproductive meetings." We agree that unfortunately there are too many endless and unproductive meetings. However, from the point of view of a practicing manager, not an outside observer, productive meetings are foremost among the significant activities through which management can accomplishes its task. Because he thinks that meetings can be so valuable, Dr. Andrew Grove, the previous CEO of Intel and now its Chairman of the Board, and the winner of Time's Man of the Year, 1997, in his outstanding book, *High Productivity Management*, writes frequently on the use of management meetings as an indispensable management tool.

Meetings-good, bad, or otherwise-occur in all organizations, regardless of structure. To suggest useless meetings are unique to a hierarchical structure is ludicrous. If Mr. Gordon really wants to observe some "endless" and "unproductive" sessions, he should sit in on a few new age-style team meetings.

It seems that those who advocate changes in organizational structure will lay nearly every organizational problem on the existing structure. For example, they say if you are working in a hierarchy, you may be facing the following issues:

* Managers make decisions in a vacuum without consulting those closest to the problem.

* Once the "bugs are worked out," work rules, norms, and procedures become resistant to change.

* Job descriptions are over-specialized, creating inefficiencies and mindless boredom.

* Departments fail to communicate with one another.

* Managers tend to hire and promote people like themselves, failing to value diversity.

* Job procedures, job descriptions, and working relationships are rammed down peoples' throats by top management.

* The stifling bureaucratic atmosphere drives out creative, independent individuals.

*People without value-added roles create useless "busywork" for themselves.

* Rewards are based on one's seniority or rank, or on the boss' favoritism, rather than on meaningful contributions to important goals.

The obvious question is what do these have to do with hierarchies? None of the statements represent a deficiency in the management structure or problems that are inherent in the form. It is as true with a hierarchy as it is with every conceivable organizational structure that its effectiveness is a direct function of how well it is managed. As mentioned earlier, poor management will cause any structure to fail.

Perhaps somewhere in the universe there is an organization that has no hierarchy, no boss-subordinate relationships, no individuals with authority and power over anyone else, no one who gives orders when orders are needed, no decision-making process other than consensus, and where individuals march to their own beat. If such an organization exists, its life span can be counted in months or it exists as a paper fantasy of a consultant or management theorist waiting for the next gullible CEO to share the fantasy and pay for it. There is not an organization in this country that is not fundamentally organized with a hierarchical structure, the existence of team, concentric, or upside-down organization charts not withstanding. Human nature being what it is, a pecking order, no matter how informal, is a fundamental part of the dynamics of any group, including self-managed, supposedly autonomous work teams.

WHY THE HIERARCHY WORKS

Despite the many challenges and the continuous attacks on its integrity, the hierarchy continues to flourish as the predominate structure in all types and sizes of organizations. Why hierarchies do not work has been a persistent topic in the management literature, particularly in the past decade; why they do work has received little attention in print. Perhaps the topic is not exciting enough. Perhaps it doesn't require substantial change at a time when change is revered. Perhaps it's too traditional for the new age theorists. Or perhaps its simplicity does not fit the model of chaos, confusion, and turmoil that keeps management consultants in business.

Hierarchies work for following reasons:

1. There is little ambiguity in terms of lines of communication, authority, and accountability. The simplicity and symmetry of hierarchical structures make them easy to understand. The confusion and anxiety resulting from unclear reporting relationships and lack of direction are minimized. People know how and where to go to get things done.

2. They provide a clear sense of identity for employees by establishing the various units with which they identify. Divisions, departments, agencies, and sections - all are units that provide membership and serve as a form of personal identification.

3. Divisions and groups produce a comfort level for workers by following a pattern that surrounds us in many aspects of life - in nature, at home, in schools, clubs, and social organizations.

A fascinating story is told in *Beyond the Hype* about ICCG (a division of Allen Bradley). The CEO of ICCG had come from the field of consulting where he had attempted to change the organizational structure of his client companies. When he had the chance to do it in his own company he changed the structure two times, each without any improvement in results while creating new and more difficult problems. Finally he came up with the "Concentric" structure. In concentric structure every work unit is in a circular design without any lines of authority of a regular and typical organization chart. The purpose was to show the cross-functional nature of the work. As the authors report: "In practice, it turned out, the many ambiguities of maintaining a team-based organization had simply led to the introduction of new formal procedures for control-although nobody had yet learned to call them bureaucratic." He might have said, had he realized it, that human nature is simply taking its course by beginning to assert a natural hierarchy.

ICCG's experience is not unique. When the team concept was first introduced during the TQM era, the prevailing implementation process produced a structure that was (and still is in many companies) as cumbersome and bureaucratic as they come-the lumbering dinosaur, dressed in new clothes. Teams reported to a Quality Committee that reported to a Quality Council that reported to a Steering Committee-a hierarchy of committees that contributed significantly to the early demise of the team concept in many organizations. Add to these committees new company policies covering all aspects of teaming, ground rules, agendas, minutes, proposal procedures, and approval processes and the bureaucracy grows very quickly. The irony is that the operating organization-a hierarchy- continued to plug along, doing the business of the company.

Eccles and Nohria conclude that "The ICCG story is an important lesson for those who believe that cross-functional teams-or 'super teams' as they are sometimes called-offer the ultimate structural panacea that will break through bureaucracy's iron cage and deliver us into a new age of egalitarian management."

Most of the "new management" writers don't know that the "team" concept is not new. It has been tried before with little success. A classic example occurred in the 1960s in a company called Non-Linear Systems. This company, located in Del Mar, California, implemented a team approach very similar to today's self-managed work teams. Each team consisted of six to eight people with a technician as the team leader. The teams were given complete responsibility to perform their respective tasks, with team members deciding who would perform what activities. The only requirement was that the job "must pass rigorous quality control and meet customer specifications."

This company was written up in every newspaper and journal and glorified in the mainstream business magazines. Articles appeared in Harvard Business Review, for example, maintaining that Non-Linear Systems' team approach was the prototype of future organizations. There was a long waiting list of people who wanted to join the company and work in a "democratic" organization.

The President and seven Vice Presidents comprised the Executive Council. They defined their job as counseling the teams to achieve their objective.

In the mid 1970s this "democratic" company with all its teamwork had to declare bankruptcy-not Chapter 11, but Chapter 7. There were no articles written about the causes of the failure of this company. The only announcement was a one-paragraph statement about the bankruptcy in the Los Angeles Times. Those who praised the company would not admit their failure to understand the fundamental differences between social democracy and business democracy.

Another lesson to learn from the so called " worker democracy" is the story of Harman Automotive Inc. in Bolivar, Tennessee. This company, as Barnaby J. Fedder (The New York Times, February 21, 1998) reports, "was internationally renowned as the site of an audacious experiment in worker empowerment." Thousands of representatives from other companies made the trek to see how Harman ran the organization. Universities, federal government, and organizations such as the Ford Foundation spent millions of dollars observing and documenting the Harman concept. Harman employees were traveling around the country, spreading the Harman gospel. Over time, the visits and the trips interfered so much with company operation that the activities had to be curtailed.

Although empowerment is an important concept and has been implemented successfully in a number of organizations, Harman fell victim to the most common reason for failure in creating an empowered organization. Sidney Harman himself said it best when he concluded, "We were too idealistic. I didn't recognize soon enough how critical a role the managers have to play. You don't go anywhere unless you get those guys to passionately sign on." Mr. Harman ignored one of the fundamentals of organizations: managers, not CEOs, manage the organization.

"Lacking the training," writes Fedder, "and in many cases the will to lead without commanding, Harman's managers were in over their heads once key groups of workers decided to use their new freedom mainly to create opportunities to leave work early."

Michael Maccoby, a Washington-based consultant,

was given the assignment by Harman and the UAW to design and coordinate the Bolivar Project. It seems that Mr. Maccoby was not only "too idealistic," but his efforts were also carried out without any realistic and logical understanding of organizational requirements. Mr. Maccoby is not unlike the social experimenters whose New Age theories obscure rational judgment. Any organization that does not practice the fundamentals well or abandons them in the implementation of new theory is doomed to fail. Among those fundamentals is that new organizational initiatives must be managed into an organization. They will not happen simply because the CEO-as Mr. Harman learned-says they will.

Harman Automotive, Inc. was shut down in February 1998.

One of the major fundamentals of business is accepting hierarchy as a realistic and practical way to operate an organization. The question is not whether we want hierarchy or not-there is no realistic choice. The question is how we want to operate that hierarchy. If we use the hierarchy as an autocratic pecking order or a command and control structure, it's not only being misused but abused. If, on the other hand, it is structured as a hierarchy of knowledge with unique accountabilities and limitations at each level, clearly defined and reinforced, then not only do we have a secure organizational base but we also have an environment in which testing and implementation of new theories can be successfully accomplished.

Frederick G. Hilmer and Lex Donaldson from the Australian Graduate School of Management at the University of New South Wales are among the few scholars who argue against new age approaches to management (Strategic Direction, July/August 1997.) Their research indicated that the so-called flat versus structured organizations are not producing any better results than the hierarchical ones. In large organizations, they believe the delivery of products and services require careful analysis and planning. And since most organizations are complex and diverse, Hilmer and Donaldson concluded that a streamlined hierarchy is the most effective organizational structure.

THE HIERARCHY OF KNOWLEDGE

In the current business literature, statements in support of hierarchies are looked upon as being "old fashioned," dictatorial, and passé (as though business, like fashions, must change every year.) The hierarchy of knowledge as presented in this book and fully explained in subsequent chapters, is far from the command-and-control structure by which hierarchies are so often negatively characterized and to which its detractors so vehemently object. The hierarchy of knowledge, while preserving the integrity of the organizational structure, also emphasizes the need for each level of the hierarchy to possess specific knowledge and skills that are unique to that level. Implementation of this hierarchical concept is the most effective way to assure the integrity of organizational structure and to prevent a hierarchy from becoming a lumbering bureaucracy.

Above all else, properly structured hierarchies work because of a logical tiering of knowledge. Any organization - because it is foremost an occupational association and not simply a collection of autonomous individuals - must be staffed by those who perform four general functions:

1. Employees, who produce, sell, and deliver the product or service from which revenue is derived, or that is required by the organization's charter;

2. Supervisors, who oversee the work by providing the support and resources necessary to produce the product or service;

3. Managers, who implement the infrastructure,

procedures, and policies by which the organization is to function; and,

4. Top management, who provide for the long-term growth and development of the entire organization.

Each of these functions requires specialized knowledge(s) that are unique to each function and that must be applied in hierarchical order, either bottom up or top down. That is not to say that there are not commonalties of knowledge that exist at all levels. Certainly there is a base level of knowledge about the company-its products, structure, policies, and missions-that all employees should have. Of course, some employees in any function of the organization may have extensive knowledge about any of the other functions. A sales manager, whose primary function is to manage the sales group, may have had experience in customer service, in supervising a sales force, and in direct sales. Thus, he or she may have expertise in a number of organizational functions. "Coming up through the ranks," means moving from one hierarchical function to the next, thus bringing accumulated knowledge of each level as the upward moves are made.

The key concept to keep in mind is that along with common knowledge, each functional level requires knowledge that is both unique to that level and independent of all other levels. Successful athletic teams exemplify this concept perfectly. While all players on the field must have a set of common skills regardless of their position on the team, each also must bring a skill and knowledge set that is specific to that position. If the players on a football team carried out only the skills or knowledge that they have in common-running, blocking, and tackling, knowing the rules-their win-loss percentage would be nothing to shout about. What does a quarterback get paid for that nobody else gets paid for? A center? A place-kicker? How about the coach? Is there specialized knowledge required? What about the general manager or athletic director? Again, is specialized knowledge required? In all cases the answer is a resounding "Yes!"

The company "team" is no different, with one critical exception. And this exception exemplifies a common flaw found in many hierarchies. Football players are generally not promoted from one position to another and can develop and hone their skills over extended periods of time. Thus, they get better and better at their specialized function. Companies "players," on the other hand, are promoted to new positions, often well before they have fully developed their specialized skills, or, worse yet, at a time when their specialized knowledge and skills are providing a major contribution to the organization from the position they are in. The best salesperson gets promoted to sales manager. The average salesperson often gets promoted to sales supervisor - the former on the basis of "no where else to go" at the sales level; the latter on the basis that he or she "can't sell very well but has great people skills."

Either employee has a chance at succeeding as a sales supervisor or sales manager if they are able to learn the specialized knowledge required. Both will more than likely fail because it is often wrongly assumed that supervision is only an extension of the function below it. One supervisor described his promotion to supervision as nothing more than "giving up overtime pay." Many managers are nothing more than grown-up supervisors, having been told that managing is the same as supervising except that you do it for more people and more than one department. Top executives often micro-manage, not because they want to, but because they don't know any better. That is, they entered top management with only the knowledge of the functions they used to perform and never attained the knowledge and skills unique to top management.

The obscene bloating of management ranks that occurred during the decades of the 1960s and 1970s is a direct result of "managing through commonality." While each function demands specialized knowledge, no specialized training was provided or required as promotions occurred. These were the decades of humanistic management in which it was assumed if management people had good people skills, they could supervise and manage anything or anybody. Billions of dollars were spent on training in interpersonal skills. The net result was that everyone got along but the work suffered or simply didn't get done. More specialized staff functions were added because the knowledge required to carry these specialized functions did not exist where it should-in the operating environment. Many new layers of supervision were added-lead workers, senior operators, associate supervisors, foremen, superintendents-on the basis that the supervisors did not have the expertise required. Middle management ranks swelled because middle managers were focused on both the product or the service that was being produced several levels below them, and with the cumbersome levels of supervision that existed.

Did hierarchies become lumbering dinosaurs? Absolutely. However, a lumbering dinosaur hierarchy is testament to its size not to its structure. Slowness of foot and, conversely, agility and flexibility, are functions more of the integrity of the body structure. A hierarchy with multiple layers of management may indeed become a lumbering dinosaur. An unacceptably slow and cumbersome entity arises when communication must flow through too many layers, each of which makes an addition or alteration in some way. The result can be a grotesquely obese form that cannot be adequately supported by its underlying structure. In truth, hierarchies are mismanaged into bureaucracies and bureaucracies become the lumbering dinosaurs.

In our view, lean and mean is now the name of the game. Organizations must be prepared to react to the changing needs of a fast-paced business environment. Your customers must be served faster and better than the competition's. Your company must be poised to respond in a nanosecond to the opportunities and demands of the Information Age.

The time has come to break up the cumbersome hierarchies. Time to create smaller profit centers and business units that are mobile, flexible, and fast afoot. Time to put a hard-charging vice president in charge, give him or her two fast-track managers, three or four supervisors, a lean operating crew, and all the support each needs from corporate. Plus time to give them a long-range plan, complete P&L accountability, and performance goals. Only then will you have successfully dismantled your unwieldy hierarchy into a series of smaller, more efficient hierarchies, all securely and smartly connected to the corporate hierarchy. The dinosaur becomes a jaguar with an underlying structure of strength and speed.

How long will these "new hierarchies" stay lean and mean? That depends on whether your organization has incorporated the hierarchy of knowledge or not. Because without each "little hierarchy" doing what it must do, without the existence of the specialized knowledge(s) being properly applied at each appropriate level, and at the appropriate time, the history of impetuous bureaucratic growth will almost assuredly repeat itself, and a new species of dinosaur will ultimately appear.

The hierarchy of knowledge is fundamental to the success of the organization because it is basic to the organization. All other approaches of the last two decades have provided, at best, short periods of success but were ultimately unsustainable. In 1982 Thomas J. Peters and Robert H. Waterman Jr. wrote *In Search of Excellence,* a best seller that caught the public's attention and popularized the reading of books on management. In that book the authors identified forty-three companies that were rated as "excellent" based on eight attributes identified by the authors as the keys to excellence.

That was in 1982. In 1984, just two years later, Business Week in its November 5, 1984 cover story indicated that fourteen out of the forty-three companies no longer exhibited those critical attributes. How critical could those attributes be if they can endure no longer than two years? After a speech by Peters at Hewlett-Packard, a division manager told him: "What we should do is call you in to give a speech once a quarter. So we can remember what it was that we were when we were really a great company." If the senior management of an organization does not remember what they did to be a great company, then the attributes given by an outsider on a purely intellectual basis are worthless.

THE LEVELS OF DISCONTINUITY

Within the remaining chapters of this book we will give a more detailed description of the hierarchy of knowledge. The hierarchy is based on a concept that we have termed "The Levels of Discontinuity." Indeed, a major characteristic of the hierarchy of knowledge is its discontinuity. This means that the specialized knowledge required by successful supervisors is not simply the continuation of the knowledge and skills obtained in a non-supervisory position, although those previous skills and knowledge are important as background for the new set of skills required in supervision. This is a major reason why the change to supervisor is often traumatic for the individual. Because they must discontinue what may have been years of skills learned as employees and performers in order to learn new and unique supervisory skills from scratch.

One major reason that supervision has deteriorated as a management position over the years is that many supervisors are promoted because they are outstanding performers at the employee level. And rather than becoming full-fledged supervisors, they continue to do the work they already know and which got them promoted and, for the most part, management encourages them to do so, allowing the act of supervising to take a back seat. The net result is that the job of supervisor is performed at best halfheartedly or, at worst, automatically falls to the first level of middle management.

Very often, an even more visible example of discontinuity occurs when supervisors are promoted to middle management. The supervisor, who doesn't realize that this entry into a management position requires learning new organization management skills, will tend to concentrate more on what he or she is more comfortable with-supervision. The net result is a double-edged management problem. The next level of management is pulled down to do the manager's job, and as you might predict, the new manager usurps the supervisor's job. What happens? Neither job gets done well, and the organization loses a good supervisor and gains a poor manager in the process. It's easy to see how management levels can multiply beyond the capacity of an organization to support them. Moving from middle management into an executive management position creates the next level of discontinuity. Senior management requires specific sets of skills for which there is little preparation as one moves up through the ranks. Each level of management (below senior management) requires specialized skills and knowledge(s). Together these levels perform the function of internal management-that is, running the organization on a day-to-day basis. Senior management, on the other hand, is accountable for external management: focusing on the long-term growth, development, and perpetuation of the organization. The senior executive who does not recognize the need for external focus and does not develop the specialized skills required is destined to continue focusing internally. Not only does the integrity of the organizational structure suffer, but also the future of the organization, in an ever-changing business climate, is put at risk.

CHAPTER 4

THE MISSION WORKER

The Most Significant Level of Employee

A discussion of the characteristics of a successful organization usually starts with all the glowing attributes of leadership at the top. After all, success begins and ends, at least in the minds of some management pundits, with the captain of industry piloting his or her ship with a sure hand through smooth and rough waters.

This chapter begins at the other end of the organization where the work is accomplished, where the product is made or the service delivered, and where most of the resources and energy of a successful organization are focused. We're going to begin with the workers, the employees, the craftspeople, the associates, the members of the cast or - as we're going to call them - the mission workers.

To the best of our knowledge, the term "mission worker" was first used by Frank Hoffman, co-founder of Practical Management Inc. Mr. Hoffman coined the term to denote a special group of people in an organization. He started using the term more than thirty years ago in a seminar titled "Successful Middle Management." Today this term and many of the concepts covered in that seminar have taken on even more significance.

Basically, the term mission worker refers to the people who actually accomplish the mission of a work unit. Regardless of their background, skills, educational level, or pay rates, if they are paid to accomplish the mission of a given unit or department within an organization, they are mission workers.

For example, in an accounting unit where the mission is to produce financial documents, accountants are the mission workers, as are the accounts receivable clerks and the bookkeepers, regardless of how many degrees they may have or how skilled they may be. Assembly workers, machine operators, nurses, surgeons, customer service reps, salespeople, reservations agents, pilots-all qualify as mission workers. Salary, educational level, and title or position has no bearing on this definition. On a surgical team, the primary mission worker is the surgeon; in a research lab, a Ph.D. chemist may be the primary mission worker. Both can hardly be called poorly educated and lowly paid. Thus, brain surgeons to bricklayers, attorneys to electricians, all are mission workers.

Mission workers then can exist anywhere within an organizational structure, not just at the bottom of the chart. Those at the top of an organization chart, such as vice presidents of economic research or of long-range planning, assuming they actually spend significant time doing the research and the planning, are mission workers. Vice presidents in any department might have mission workers reporting to them. As will be true throughout our discussion of organizational positions, the critical factor is the relationship to the work, not the position on the organization chart.

What is the significance of the term, mission workers? It is simply that these two words define both the structure and the performance of the organization. Mission workers are by far the most significant group of people in the entire organization. They bring to the organization the specialized skills to produce the products or services that are the lifeblood of the company. Without mission workers, supervisors, managers, executives and even CEOs are superfluous. Since organizations exist solely to produce the mission work, they are the true heroes of any successful business entity.

There are other critical reasons why organizations must give the mission work level significantly more attention and support than has traditionally been the case.

1. Mission workers utilize and, to a large extent, control the greatest percentage of total resources expended by the organization. Raw materials, machine utilization and maintenance, transportation and distribution, utilities, construction, paperwork and processes-all, and many more, are directly expended or impacted by mission workers. How well they handle these enormous responsibilities directly effects the overall survival of the organization. And as we will state many times and in many ways, how well mission workers perform is a direct reflection of how well management carries out its unique and specific functions.

2. Mission workers embody the history, the culture, and the accumulated knowledge of the organization. Collectively, they have lived (and often suffered) through all the operational, production, and technological changes the company has endured. By their performance over time, they have set the standards for productivity, quality, costs, and safety. They have developed and maintained the levels of behavior and the unique character, the culture, of the company. Among them, they possess the intricate and detailed knowledge of the products, the services, and the operational processes and idiosyncrasies that are nowhere to be found in the operating manuals and training programs. In their heads is indispensable knowledge that exists nowhere else in the organization. They are the knowledge workers in the new trend toward learning organizations.

3. Mission workers are the "face" of the organization. They are the organization in the eyes of the customer, not only in direct customer contact, but because their work is what the customer buys. The satisfaction of the customer, and thus the reputation

and perpetuation of the organization, is with the company's product or service. It's the mission worker's name that is stamped on the inside of that tire or on the bottom of that grocery bag. They bring those products to market from raw material to finished product, and management would do well to remember that.

There can be no question that the stability, security, and continual development of the workforce are the most important factors in the stability of the entire organization. Assuming strong supervision, an organization with a strong base can continue to function successfully regardless of the upheavals that are caused by management changes, the fads of the day, and other forms of chaos perpetuated by the denizens of mahogany row. Management can jerk the organization around all it wants to but, if strong supervision and a stable workforce are not weakened in the process, the day-to-day business will continue to be accomplished.

Unfortunately, management in many organizations has not learned its lesson over the years. Mission workers are very often the targets of management's efforts to "improve the performance of the organization" or in today's world "to produce a greater return for investors and shareholders," including themselves. The emphasis on short-term returns has made heroes of many top executives while seriously degrading and weakening the structure upon which the organization is built. As good as the economy appears at the time of the writing of this book, the trend toward the degradation of the mission work level poses a serious threat to the long-term performance of many companies.

In what ways is this degradation occurring?

1. The most obvious one is downsizing. The enormous number of lay-offs that started in the 1980s and continues today, despite the strong economy, is

unprecedented. And those people go out the door with a vast store of accumulated knowledge, skill, and expertise. These are irreplaceable resources, which in both the short-term and the long-term, are a much greater loss than the gains made in cost reductions. It is particularly disheartening to note that there is rarely any attempt by downsizing organizations to differentiate between the talent and the deadwood. Cuts are made across the board, or by function/department, or by offering a leave package that those who have the greatest number of years-and thus experience and expertise-will be the most likely to accept. Add to that the threat that if not enough people take the leave package, terminations will be arbitrarily made until the magic cost savings had been reached.

2. Replacing the more experienced, more qualified mission workers has resulted in an influx of lower-paid, less qualified replacements. Their inability to perform at a high level of productivity or quality is evident in the current deterioration of consumer satisfaction with levels of quality and service.

3. Fewer mission workers are being required to complete more mission work in less time. Further cost savings were accomplished by companies that either hired fewer replacements than those laid off or, more likely, did not hire any replacements at all, electing to spread the existing mission work to those who remained. Productivity, cost and other performance requirements were not changed to reflect the lowered capabilities. Thus, time becomes a most critical resource as a reduced force of mission workers push harder to produce an equal or greater amount of work. The eight-hour day has become a thing of the past. More work, less pay, more stress,

less downtime, and never-ending work is a formula for disaster.

4. Leadership has been seriously eroded, particularly at the supervisory level. Younger workers with little or no mission work or leadership experience are being promoted into supervisory positions, often because they have a college degree or are considered "fast trackers." Little regard is paid to the effect on the work itself as well as the morale, the confidence, and the continued development of the mission workers. Age notwithstanding, supervisors often have a negative impact on the mission work because in many instances they spend more time doing the work of their employees than they do supervising. Although there are circumstances in which a supervisor may perform mission work for legitimate reasons, supervisors usually perform such tasks because:

*they are familiar with the mission worker's job, but they don't know what to do as supervisors;

*they dislike the whole idea of supervising and have accepted the job because it pays more than the mission worker's salary;

*they really don't realize that they are doing something they should not be doing on a regular basis. While more mission work may be accomplished in the short term, the absence of leadership at the supervisory level will most certainly, over time, degrade both the mission work and the mission workers.

5. The team movement, while designed to improve the overall performance and personal gratification

of the mission workers, has often had the opposite effect. Due mainly to ill-conceived strategies for implementation and nurturing of a team environment, the net result of the team movement in many organizations has been an enormous waste of resources, distrust of management and its motives, and serious issues related to accountability.

There is little doubt that companies which cater solely to investors, stockholders, and Wall Street are seriously neglecting those who produce the products and services that keeps the companies in business. External influences are critical to the success of any organization and top management should spend a great deal of their time responding to these influences. However, the equilibrium of the organization is equally dependent upon successful management of the internal, day-to-day operation of the organization. Continuously maintaining and improving the performance of the mission work is of highest priority in managing the internal organization. Middle managers, supervisors and mission workers are the key players in running the organization internally.

The next two chapters will be devoted to internal management, focusing primarily on the unique accountabilities of each level. In a nutshell, mission workers are accountable for getting the work out, supervisors for seeing that it gets out, and managers for assuring that it can get out.

By clearly defining the mission worker we can discover whose job it is to do what within the internal organization. Perhaps even more pertinent, we can determine who should not be doing the critical tasks of the mission work.

Perhaps the persistent confusion existing between mission worker and supervisor best explains why there is rarely true management in a hospital, in a scientific unit, or in the running of a university. In a hospital, the best surgeon usually becomes the head of surgery. But the surgeon still performs surgery on a regular basis. In effect, the surgeon continues to function as a highly qualified mission worker, not a true supervisor or a manager. At best, the surgeon performs perfunctory administrative duties for the surgical unit simply because surgical management demands a great deal of non-mission work. It demands time the head of surgery simply does not have.

In a scientific unit, chief scientists conduct experiments. In a university, most department heads go right on teaching. No matter how hard these organizations try, and they have tried for decades, true managing cannot be performed in these units unless they change their way of doing business. And what would that mean? Simply that the best surgeon could no longer perform surgery, the best scientist could no longer experiment in his or her chosen scientific field, and the best professors, who have become department heads, could not teach or take the time to publish. The irony of this situation is that no one-the supervisor or the mission workers-really benefits. The supervisor does very little supervision; the mission workers get little or no supervision. Neither gets better at what they are doing except by practice and individual effort.

REVITALIZING THE MISSION WORKER - A SURVIVAL NEED

Organizations must regenerate the passion and loyalty that once earned American business the position of pre-eminence in world markets. The place to start is where it all happens, where the mission work of the organization gets done. The revival of mission workers as a major force in today's business environment may well be the most important factor in the revitalization of American industry. To do so will require some substantial changes in the way many organizations are managed.

Return to the Fundamentals

Begin by recognizing that the average mission worker is conscientious, dedicated, and willing to work as hard as necessary to accomplish the goals that are set out for them. A primary responsibility of any organization is to make it possible for mission workers to do what they already are motivated to do. Managers and supervisors who live by that credo will spend the better part of their working day making sure that the work environment-not just the workers-is free of the obstacles and roadblocks that so often stand in the way of sustaining continuous, high level efforts to accomplish productive work.

What happens is that the most important work of any organization is somehow sabotaged by one or more obstacles placed squarely in the path of the mission workers. Sometimes these obstacles are the result of well meaning efforts to help, insensitivity to the existence of obstacles, lack of awareness of the consequences of programs designed to encourage greater performance by the mission worker, or ineffective leaders who demand performance despite the obstacles and shrug off mission workers' concerns.

Most operating problems are the result of deficiencies in the process, the work environment, or resources. Yet, in most cases, the finger of blame is pointed first at the mission worker. Conventional wisdom has been, "fix the employee and you fix the problem." Since most of the causes of operating problems are external to the employees, "fixing" them does nothing but cost money or embitter the employee, while the operating problem remains. How many millions of training dollars have been wasted in just such a scenario?

Moran and Bailey of Sibson and Company stated in a 1993 newspaper article, "Employees are cynical and angry about the constant parade of initiatives that come with the usual pronouncements of imminent importance-Program of the Month, quality initiatives, employee involvement programs, suggestion programs, customer service programs."

In addition, employees who are still struggling to accomplish what they get paid for, who do not know what is expected of them, who need job coaching, who hold two jobs to make ends meet, who haven't talked to a supervisor in weeks, are being subjected to teamwork training and endless team meetings, "seven habits" lectures, imprinting and affirmation seminars, and right-brain left-brain training. Its no wonder mission workers view these programs as a waste of precious resources that could be far better used to hire more help, train supervisors, buy a new truck or replace out-dated equipment.

Returning to the fundamentals is nothing more than giving the mission workers the respect they deserve and, with it, the time, effort and resources to help them make their optimum contribution to the company. That, fair compensation, a sense of security, and a little recognition now and then is all they really want. With the basics covered, even a dash of the "seven habits" or an affirmation statement or two might be welcomed.

Provide A Compensation System That Works

Since nearly the beginning of time, organizations have struggled with designing a performance appraisal and compensation system that truly appraises performance and provides equitable compensation for that performance. As practiced by most organizations, neither mission workers nor supervisors look forward to the annual or semi-annual performance appraisal sessions. They are perceived by supervisors as little more than a ritual-a game of "going through the motions"-and by the mission worker as a right of passage to the next pay level. Neither party considers the outcome meaningful in terms of future performance.

A major indicator that performance appraisal is a problem area is that, since the concept was introduced by

General Electric more than sixty years ago, almost every company has changed the system at least every three years.

    The first problem with performance appraisals is the term itself. Appraisal is by definition a backward-looking process. Only that which was, or is, can be appraised. Yet, the objective of performance appraisals, written right into the policy itself, is to improve performance. While current and past performance must be appraised in order to improve it, the emphasis typically is on what went well or what didn't go so well during the past six to twelve months. Assuming decisions about pay raises will be based on the appraisal, the past becomes considerably more important to the mission worker than the future. If performance of the mission worker was positive and a pay raise more than likely imminent, then discussing how to improve the performance is a comfortable, but perhaps fleeting, discussion. If past performance was unsatisfactory and a pay raise unlikely, then any discussion of future improvement would most likely not even be heard by the mission worker, much less making a commitment to it.

    The second key problem with performance appraisal systems is that often they are not really designed as tools for performance appraisal. They are often catch-alls, recording, but not limited to, past performance, future improvements, salary rates and salary increases or decreases, performance strengths and weaknesses, performance improvement plans, training needed, and future goals and aspirations. But to cut to the chase, performance appraisal systems are often designed for salary administration purposes and for adherence to an overall, one-size-fits-all compensation plan. Mixing these two issues, among others, creates a volatile combination that satisfies no one but the Human Resources Department. Designing a process to satisfy several different but remotely related objectives rarely works. All-purpose tools are nice in concept but falter in execution. A Swiss Army Knife has its uses, but not as a substitute for a real knife, screwdriver, bottle opener, and scissors. If Human Resources designs the form and is also accountable for salary administration and general compensation, it's a fair bet that the appraisal system will be skewed pretty heavily in that direction, with performance appraisal and compensation decisions at the supervisor-mission work levels taking a back seat.

What happens to most performance appraisal forms, particularly those designed and disseminated by Human Resources? They are reviewed by the Human Resources Department for both form and substance. This concept alone makes what is written on the form invalid. Supervisors know that as they evaluate the mission workers on these forms, they themselves are also being evaluated by what is written on the form. It is not unusual for Human Resource Departments to change a supervisor's salary recommendations based on the form alone and on compensation policy. Supervisors and mission worker soon discover the real world and begin to skew the appraisal based on third party evaluation, rather than on true merit and performance. This third party evaluation of performance creates nothing but resentment on the part of both the mission worker and the supervisor.

The third major problem with performance appraisals is that they are conducted formally and only once or twice a year. Job performance, on the other hand, takes place on a daily basis. Thus, the potential for the formal performance appraisal to have any major impact on the mission worker's daily efforts is limited. If, as most management theorists would suggest, supervisors and mission workers have on-going, real-time performance discussions, with documentation and plans for improving real-time issues, then there would be little need for the formal appraisal sessions. Or if they were conducted would be little more than a summary of what the supervisor and mission workers have already discussed and documented. Perhaps this is too logical and too fundamental to fit in today's world of 360-degree appraisals, peer evaluations, and committee reviews.

Fix or Abandon the Team Environment

The Total Quality Management movement, so predominant in the 1980s as to qualify as a cult movement, has gone the way of all the other such movements that have dotted the history of American business. However, like most such company-wide movements, vestiges of TQM still remain, chief among them the team concept. And for good reason. Teams can be vital forces for change and the implementation of significant improvements in the productivity and overall performance of an organization.

Unfortunately, teams have not reached their potential in most organizations, not for lack of interest, efforts, or resources but because the white shirts and consultants controlled the process from beginning to end. The result has often been an admirable concept bogged down in endless meetings, reports and paperwork, overly sophisticated and time-consuming data collection, lack of accountability, management by committee, and little or no involvement by middle managers and supervisors. The cookie-cutter, one-size-fits-all approach recommended by consultants and ram-rodded by an executive steering committee so blatantly undermines the integrity of the organization structure (and the managers and supervisors therein) as to render the team concept doomed from the outset.

While the failures of the team movement are predominant, there have been a number of success stories. Why do some succeed while most fail? There are three primary reasons. Teams that share the following attributes succeed.

A. They get down to business immediately.

The cookie-cutter approach requires the establishment of a whole set of agreements, documents, logistical arrangements, and role definitions before the team can even think about working on anything of organizational value. Endless hours are devoted to mission and vision statements in which word-smithing becomes the primary agenda item-should we say we "are" or we "will be" the world leader in quality and customer service. More hours spent on ground rules, determination, definition, and establishment of team roles, minutes, agendas, and methods of communication with management. Months have now gone by and not a lick of real work has been accomplished.

Have the people who designed this team approach ever been mission workers? Do they understand that most mission workers are active people who work in a world of real-time production of critical tasks? Who in most cases are eager to improve those tasks and anxious to express their ideas? Who are assigned to a team, are excited about finally being asked to contribute, and enthused about being a part of team for that purpose?

Most mission workers bring a high level of energy and excitement to that first team meeting. But how quickly that energy is squelched by the hours-often stretching into months-required to do all the so-called team management activities required by the company manual. The energy of a team dissipates in direct proportion to the time taken to produce teamwork as opposed to real work. It's no wonder that the best mission workers lose interest early, begin to miss meetings, and eventually drop out. And the credibility of the team concept goes with them.

The most successful teams are the ones that are business-driven from the very beginning. They have a project to work on immediately-one that has been assigned or one they agree to during the first or second meeting. The team management and administrative functions are also completed but they are of secondary importance. The majority of the meeting time from the beginning is spent on their project; less time-perhaps fifteen minutes per meeting-is devoted to the secondary topics. Often, teams of this type will make such good progress on their projects that they decide mission and vision statements, ground rules, and a formal team structure have little or no relationship to their success.

B. Successful teams have a working, accountable relationship with management.

Accountability is a major problem in a team environment. Not only is it an issue within the teams themselves but also in the team's relationship with management and management's relationship with the team. It is not unlike the supervisor's role as a buffer between mission workers and upper management. Supervisors are accountable to their immediate managers for the performance of the mission workers and for representing the mission workers to their managers.

Theoretically, in a typical team environment similar accountability does not exist. Teams are often accountable to a management committee or a steering committee as opposed to an operating supervisor or manager. Directions and policies are usually determined by the committee and formal communications established between the teams and the committee. Proposals generated by the teams are presented by the teams to the committee or a designated member. Decisions are made (often after sitting in an in-basket for weeks) and, if proposals are approved, returned to the teams for implementation.

This decision-making process tends to by-pass the operating supervisors and managers. Having little or no input into the proposals or the decisions, the supervisors and managers are then held accountable for the success or failure of the implemented changes. This is a reversal of the "responsibility without authority" concept. In effect, it gives the decision-makers the authority to impose the changes but no responsibility for the consequences. It is no surprise that many managers and supervisors are often either overtly or covertly antagonistic toward the team concept.

Mission workers are also not served well by this decision-by-committee since they are denied a valuable resource in carrying out their team projects. Managers and supervisors should be an integral part of all deliberations, plans, and proposals carried out by teams in their operating areas. They must also be a source of day-by-day support in the implementation of changes and improvements generated by teams. Simply put, managers and supervisors should be accountable to management for the performance of teams and mission work teams should be accountable to their supervisors and managers for their performance as a team and as individuals on the team.

Mission workers, whether as individuals or as teams, need the resources of knowledge, objectivity, and functional accountability that only their immediate supervisors (or designated managers in the case of process teams or self-managed teams) can provide. Management by committee does not work anywhere else in organizations. Why do we assume it can work in a team environment?

C. Productive teams are motivated by the same factors that motivate the individuals within them.

Teams are, after all, a collection of individuals. As such they require the same degree of satisfaction, challenge, and achievement in a team environment as they do in carrying out their primary job functions. Too often management assumes that the team process alone is motivational since perhaps for the first time employees are given the opportunity to work together, to solve problems, to make contributions to the organization, and to be empowered to implement their ideas. At least, that's the company line in persuading employees that the team environment is the wave of the future.

The future is now. Many companies have abandoned the team concept and many others are questioning the value received from the resources invested. While there are many reasons for the team concept to lose its luster, chief among them is a failure to recognize that the hype used to sell the concept was not matched by the process by which the teams were implemented. A common complaint of many mission workers to describe the implementation process is that it is "all form and little substance."

Without substance, the motivational energy of mission workers dissipates rapidly. People at work generally tend to be driven by a desire to accomplish something that contributes to a worthwhile purpose. If either the value of the contribution or the purpose that it serves is questionable, people will tend to lose interest quickly and, at best, revert to going-through-the-motions or, at worst, actively resist the effort.

The most successful teams are the ones in which the intrinsic and extrinsic motivational factors, so well documented in management literature, are present:

1. Projects are perceived to be of value and, if successful, will make a valuable contribution to the organization. Too often, teams are given projects or are allowed to select ones that no one else wants to do or that no one else in the organization has ever been able to accomplish. Real examples of such projects are planning and carrying out the United Way Campaign, shelving stock, re-organizing an out-of-date filing system, organizing and re-arranging the literature in the company library, and cleaning the cafeteria. While these may be projects that need to be done, they certainly do not fit the description of real work that should be the mission of a team nor are they likely to be perceived by team members as contributing anything of real value.

2. Recognition of efforts and accomplishments is constant and evident. Teams need visibility. Collectively and individually, team members need to be reassured that their time and efforts are not only appreciated but also recognized on an ongoing basis. This does not refer to formal recognition processes-newsletters, reports to management, bulletin boards, "visibility rooms" and the like. One company set aside a room in their plant specifically for posting the minutes and agendas for all teams. It was called the "visibility room." The purpose was to allow all employees, management particularly, to see how the various teams were doing. A running joke among team members was that the only people who visited the room were facilitators and teams leaders who went in to update the minutes. More meaningful recognition and visibility occurs on a more informal basis. Supervisors talking casually about team activities with their employees who are team members, occasionally dropping in on team meetings for a short time, taking team members to lunch, discussing team progress with other members of management, asking about team activities during staff meetings (but not as part of the agenda), making specific offers to help when teams are struggling or need outside assistance-these are all informal but powerful motivational techniques for providing visibility and recognition from someone who counts-their supervisors.

3. Team activities are allowed to compete successfully with other operational demands. By their nature, team activities are not high on the list of anyone's priorities, particularly those of management. Despite the lip service given to the value of teams, when other more pressing issues arise, team activities are the first to go. After all, teams are not work-

ing on issues and problems that are imminent and that are equal in priority to the magnitude of problems that exist in the here and now. Tracing a lost shipment to a major customer, recovering from a computer crash, and preparing budget figures due in the boss' office today are certainly more pressing than holding a team meeting - and more pressing they should be in many instances.

Work activities in any organization are of two types. The first is routine duties. These are duties that must be done. The system demands them, the boss demands them, or the customer demands them. These are the activities that must be done and done on time or someone will be called to account.

The second is payoff activities. These are activities that if done well will result in improvements, making some aspects of work better, faster, cheaper or safer. However, unlike routine duties, payoff duties can be postponed until another day because there is no immediacy to the activity. They are not crisis-driven. In addition, payoff duties require planning and are not going to be implemented immediately. Thus their benefit will not be realized until sometime in the future.

Since the primary purpose for having teams in the first place is to create and implement improvements, creating and implementing pay-off activities is their reason for being. Thus, team members are forced to compete on a daily basis with the demands of routine activities that do-and should in many instances- take precedence over the less time-sensitive payoff activities. Dealing with a major production problem will win out over attending a team meeting, or working on a team project, every time.

Dealing successfully with the issue of priorities is a major challenge in a team environment. While routine duties have to be accomplished and crisis situations dealt with immediately, team activities must be able to coexist if teams members are to maintain the necessary level of energy and enthusiasm required to complete projects successfully. Arbitrarily and routinely sacrificing team time and resources to deal with day-to-day operating issues is a primary reason for team failure.

Dealing with priority issues and competing for company resources is a management responsibility. Team members cannot and should not make these decisions. For this reason among others, a basic tenet in developing a successful team environment is that the team concept must be managed into the organization. Teams will not work simply because top management says they will, even if all of the trappings of a team environment are readily apparent. Massive training efforts, mission and vision statements framed and under glass, newsletter articles, wholesale distribution of team minutes, top management involvement in teams-all are classic teamwork symbols but do not a team environment make.

Managing a team environment into an organization requires that managers and supervisors be as intimately involved with teams as they are with any other projects of major importance. This means providing the resources and guidance to get the teams started and then staying close enough to be aware of the team's progress. It also means providing encouragement and recognition, running interference when needed, and assuring a level playing field when the inevitable clash of priorities between team members occurs.

While reality dictates that routine duties are going to win most of the time, payoff duties have to compete successfully, and win some of the time if they are ever going to be given the priority they deserve.

Empowerment – The Buzz Word of the '90s

Arising from the team movement, but not unique to it, is another concept that is profound in theory but woefully deficient in implementation. Empowerment has risen to the top of the management lexicon and is touted as the means to tap into the knowledge and experience of mission workers. After all, who better to make mission work decisions and fix mission work problems than those who are actually doing the work? What better way to provide mission workers with the respect they deserve and with the job satisfaction they crave? No longer will the white shirts be mucking around in the day-by-day operations, forcing changes and actions that mission workers know don't have a chance of succeeding.

Empowerment is the ultimate "feel good" concept, the potential of which has been squandered by inept approaches to sell it within organizations and to live up to the hype by which it was promoted. The first problem is in the word itself. Webster's Dictionary defines empowerment as "to give power or authority to; to authorize." Many organizations did indeed take it literally, giving the impression that mission workers would have carte blanche in making decisions on a day-to-day basis. Little thought was given to preparing mission workers to be empowered, to finding out if they're ready and willing to be empowered, and discussing with them how the process might work best. Empowerment by mandate is antithetical to the concept itself.

Empowerment, correctly implemented, is nothing more or less than the age-old practice of delegation. Delegation is the process of providing the authority, tools, and resources to carry out a designated work activity. If mission workers are capable of doing the task but need guidance and preparation to do it successfully, then logic and good management practices require that they be "enabled" before they are "empowered". Training, guided experiences, and coaching are required at the very least. Empowerment, as in delegation, must be on a time continuum rather than date-specific. Rather than the typical practice of trying to overturn decades of "do as you're told" by "you can now, today, make your own decisions," empowerment, like delegation, requires that mission workers be provided first with the ability to be empowered and the confidence that they can successfully carry out the designated task.

Like the word itself, the concept upon which empowerment is based has also been inappropriately applied. "Driving decisions to the lowest possible level" is another feel-good concept that is not only widely misinterpreted but also downright dangerous. Quite obviously, the lowest possible level should not be making all decisions or even a majority of them. As we will describe in later chapters, each level of the organization has its unique areas of expertise and accountability and, therefore, should be empowered to make decision within those domains. To empower those at one level to make decisions more appropriate to another level poses a severe threat to the integrity of the organizational structure and to the quality of the work being directly affected. Thus, the concept upon which empowerment should be based is to "drive decisions to the lowest possible appropriate level."

As a general rule, management maintains the right and the accountability to determine the "whats" of the organization. Mission workers, including teams, should be prepared and then empowered to determine the "hows."

In addition, empowerment, inappropriately applied, often produces consequences that are the direct opposite of those intended. Empowerment, as with delegation, requires the authority to make decisions. Authority implies accountability, which further implies consequences. Recognition or criticism for the results of a decision or a project assignment should be afforded to those who are empowered to carry out the task or project. Mission workers and others who are empowered without being enabled may therefore suffer consequences for carrying out actions they were ill prepared to carry out. Rather than getting the respect and the job satisfaction they expected from empowerment, mission workers may well be disillusioned with the concept and reluctant to ever go down that road again.

The current trend toward downsizing, mergers, and replacing people with machines further diminishes the ability of mission workers, empowered or not, to perform to their abilities. The illusion of empowered mission workers has caused, or allowed, many companies to virtually eliminate supervision as a viable force in their management structure. There are still employees with the title of supervisor but they have often been reduced to paper-pushers, data-gatherers, report writers, or glorified mission workers. Ask salespeople in the field the last time they even saw, much less talked to, a sales supervisor for purposes other than collecting sales information, call ratios, and reports. Ask customer service reps in a call center the last time their supervisors (who may have thirty CSR's reporting to them) monitored a call and then carried out a coaching session with them. Ask any mission worker about the quality and value of their last performance appraisal.

Management's neglect of mission workers and supervisors is one of the most disturbing trends in current management practice. Being lulled by economic good times, happy investors and stockholders may well be creating a management environment that will be the Achilles' heel of many organizations. Human performance is still the backbone of the workplace in producing the products and services that fuel our economy. The machines that are taking over still need people to make them and keep them functioning. The unrelenting pressure to do more, the stress of long hours, the lack of time and energy to devote to family and social interactions, the diminishing loyalty, the anxieties about job security-all have a cumulative effect not only on the mission workers' job performance but also on their ability to contribute to their families and the broader community.

CHAPTER FIVE

SUPERVISORS: MANAGEMENT'S TECHNICAL EXPERTS

Supervision, done effectively, is the most difficult management job in any organization. It is also the most important in accomplishing day-to-day operating goals.

Unfortunately, the role of the supervisor has often been misunderstood over the past two decades, and its importance has been overlooked. Many organizations have actually worked hard, however inadvertently, to make it even more difficult for supervisors to supervise effectively. Although very little is published about this sore subject, the organizational senselessness that has stubbornly crept into American business can be linked directly to a decline in supervision-a decline in terms of both the position's stature and contribution to an organization.

Supervision is the very foundation of management. The supervisory level is where things are made to happen, for better or for worse. Try as they may-and all too many have tried in recent years-organizations cannot and should not eliminate this hierarchical level. Whether you call them supervisors, team leaders, crew leaders, chiefs, or coaches, this first tier of management is critical to the success of the organization. This level of management not only should remain in place, but also should be accorded renewed respect and decision-making authority. It is nearly impossible to effectively empower mission workers without first strengthening and empowering supervisors.

THE WHO AND WHY OF SUPERVISION

Who are the supervisors? Simply put, they are all of those people in the organization who have mission workers reporting directly to them. Regardless of the title, if they fit that definition and if the people reporting to them fit the definition of mission workers, then they are indeed supervisors.

Sales managers who have salespeople reporting to them are supervisors; Vice Presidents who have systems analysts reporting to them are supervisors. Supervision should not be defined by a position on an organizational chart, but by its relationship to the mission work. Thus, supervisors can exist nearly anywhere on an organizational chart. In a team environment, a team composed primarily of mission workers, working on mission work projects, should be responsible to someone in management. That "someone" is, by definition, the supervisor of that particular work project.

What makes supervision so important and unique as to warrant a special place on the management team? First: supervisors are front-line representatives of both management and the employees; they play a delicate buffer role. Second: they have significant influence on all the major resources of the organization; supervisors influence the mission workers, and the costs of the goods and services that are the lifeline of any company. Third: they are the members of the management team who are closest to the work and subsequently the most knowledgeable about it.

Therefore, it is clear that supervisors should be the primary decision-makers in mission work, operating issues, and operating problems. Organizations that de-value, ignore, or eliminate this level are running a long-term risk of the highest order.

THE UNIQUE ROLE OF SUPERVISION

To perform supervision effectively requires far more than the basic collection of good human relation's attributes that now dominate most competency lists for supervisors. It requires far more than the proverbial "Seven Habits" and the coaching and facilitating skills that now seem to dominate the training curricula for supervisors. All these may help the supervisor to be a better people person (they are important attributes, to be sure), but they are not enough to make him or her a good supervisor. The primary order of business for all supervisors is to understand their role on the management team and how that role should be played in order to make the maximum contribution to the organization.

In order to fulfill their unique position in the Hierarchy of Knowledge, supervisors must first master the main and most critical function: to be knowledgeable and concerned with all the methods and techniques by which the mission workers accomplish their mission. Without mastering these most critical elements, the supervisor will resemble a driver who is well versed in the traffic laws, but does not know how to drive a car. Such a driver has about as much value as the supervisors who talk a good game about supervision, who know all the latest theories about supervision, but can't perform it.

Mastering the methods and techniques will familiarize the supervisor with two critical areas: prevention and improvement-prevention of mission work errors, and improvement of the performance of the mission workers. Without general knowledge of methods and techniques (not necessarily the intricate details, not the nuts and bolts of the mission work), the best a supervisor can do is catch errors after they occur, often when it's too late. Similarly, improvement of mission work performance suffers when the supervisor lacks the mission work knowledge to offer good coaching and training and to achieve superior results.

A supervisor must not only be interested in work improvements but obsessed with continuous improvement in all of the methods and techniques of the mission worker's job. A supervisor must have the time to search out and learn new approaches to be used in improving the mission workers' tasks. The supervisor should experiment with new methods and should be the one who takes the lead in teaching new methods to his or her group of mission workers. That is the only way continuous improvement makes sense and is practical. A supervisor must be the critical person involved in seeing that today's job gets done today and that tomorrow's job will be even better in quality while taking less time and with lower cost. No other position or function in the organization can make these improvements continuously, realistically, practically, and successfully.

If the organization doesn't train the supervisor in the appropriate skills and does not allow the supervisor to be the pivotal force in all matters related to the mission worker, then true supervision will not take place. Subsequently, the organization will have to live with chaos, dissatisfaction, arbitration, unmotivated employees, and, most importantly, dissatisfied customers.

The actual experiences of a major Canadian telecommunications company may clarify the problems we have addressed to this point.

The new CEO of the company ordered the Human Resources Department to conduct a study to see why the company, the largest employer in the province, employed such a relatively low number of college graduates, especially at the management level. The study showed that traditionally supervisors were promoted from the ranks of the mission workers, most of who had learned their trades on the job after high school graduation. If they did outstanding jobs as supervisors, they were promoted to management positions. Most college graduates working for the company were in staff or service positions such as Human Resources, Planning, Accounting, Administration, Public Relations, Corporate Communication, and Government Relations.

This discovery disturbed the CEO. He subsequently determined that the organization needed to recruit a significant number of college graduates, preferably with degrees in humanities because they were more readily available. Money was never an object because the company still enjoyed the status of a monopoly. In addition, the government of Canada was happy to see this major organization hire so many humanities majors, who are the most difficult to place in the job market.

The question was what to do with them after they were hired. The answer? Place them in supervisory positions, replacing existing supervisors who were not college-educated. The recruiting effort was successful, resulting in an influx of college grads, all to be trained in a couple of weeks to replace the supervisors who had learned every aspect of the job but lacked the requisite college pedigree.

As you might guess, shortly after implementing this plan, chaos, confusion, and operational problems hit the organization. That unique breed of consultants who preach chaos as a sign of progress, and those who say, "if it ain't broke, break it," would have loved this organization.

Internally, the units started to fall apart because the new supervisors had no clue about what to do as a supervisor. In the two-week training, they were never taught the technical skills that a supervisor needs to have in order to guide, coach, and respond to all of the daily demands of the employees and the customers. Mounting problems and continuous complaints of customers forced the company to deal with this issue.

Their answer, directed by the CEO, was to have the staff specialists design a point system for each job the technicians had to perform. Then, let the supervisor evaluate the work of each technician by how many points he or she accumulated during a day, calculate it monthly, and reward the best performer quarterly. The workers who came up with the fewest points were candidates for additional training. Of course, the supervisors did not do the training since their humanities background was not helpful in deciding which wire goes with what unit.

The mission workers were very critical of these moves. Their primary complaint was that they had lost the supervisors who may not have been eloquent or articulate or may have treated them roughly, but who knew the job inside out. What's more, they belonged. The new supervisors were not only of little help but actually caused problems in many areas because they lacked even the most basic understanding of the day-to-day reality of the mission work. At best, relationships were strained; at worst, they were hostile.

The point system, developed by the staff people and then implemented by the supervisors became the straw that broke the camel's back. They felt that basing pay raises and disciplinary action on the system was unfair in general but more specifically it was inaccurate. For example, repairing a certain piece of equipment gained the same amount of points, regardless of the equipment's location. Therefore, if the equipment was close by, it could be fixed in much less time than the same equipment that might be miles away. Yet both jobs received the same points. Consequently, many employees who had to travel to reach distant sources scored lower than those employees who maintained equipment in nearby spots. Thus, they had to go for retraining because of low scores, not because they did not perform or did not know their jobs.

Another major problem was that most of the employees discovered there was no way for them to become supervisors since they were not college graduates. The majority of these technicians didn't want to become supervisors, but they wanted to have that option open to them. Their range of experience was from one to thirty years. They were not about to go to college, even though the company announced that tuition would be reimbursed if they attended college at night and passed their courses. College was not in the plans of these highly skilled technicians.

It is interesting to compare the experience of this company with the approach used by the sales units at MCI. In MCI's operation, supervisors were decision-makers as far as the performance of the mission workers was concerned. They continuously monitored the calls of all sales associates, who had been trained to conduct their sales approach based on a standard procedure. The main job of the MCI supervisors was to identify who needed further training and to provide it immediately, either by themselves, or by the training unit. Each supervisor then followed the progress of the associate's performance. If the improvement failed to take place after a specified time, the supervisor would take disciplinary action. The key factor in this process is that the supervisors were constantly aware of customer needs and were able to adjust the approaches taken by the associates on the spot. In short, they were empowered to improve the service on a daily basis. The sustained success of MCI can be attributed in part to management's understanding of the key role played by their supervisors.

In addition to being knowledgeable about the methods and the techniques of the mission work, supervisors need to master two additional skill sets, one generic, the other specific to the mission work, depending on the nature of the business.

The generic skills needed can be summed up generally as follows:

> 1. Mastery of adult learning principles and on-the-job training techniques. Supervisors need to be able to train mission workers, help them correct their mistakes, and retrain them when work methods change. This skill requires that supervisors learn how to teach effectively in both one-on-one and small groups situations;

> 2. Mastery of practical coaching techniques. This skill must be clear and basic, avoiding the theoretical and psychological nuances so common in current coaching workshops. Counseling, psychological analysis and profiling is dangerous in the hands of amateurs.

> 3. Skills in work method analysis. Such skills are

critical for supervisors because they must analyze work methods, eliminate duplication, and institute the most efficient way of getting the job done;

4. Proficiency in distributing work. The tasks of the mission workers must be evenly distributed so that production fluctuations can be accommodated and machine changeovers can be handled efficiently. Cross training should be a basic part of the supervisor's job.

There are also specific skills that each organization must identify for itself. The general areas of accountability for a supervisor, all of which must be followed by an action plan, are:

1. Work scheduling: duties that deal with informing the mission workers in each unit of increased or decreased work loads, work schedules, work deadlines and, when they occur, work emergencies;

2. Assurance of work's quality, accuracy, and level of service: reviewing all work quality and accuracy continuously with the mission workers;

3. Work assignments: making sure that everyone is trained and capable of doing the assigned job:

4. Handling personnel matters: interviewing, hiring, and disciplinary actions as required by the company's human resources policies;

5. Orientation and training: reviewing the performances of all the mission workers, especially the new employees, and taking appropriate action to correct skill deficiencies;

6. Cost reduction and productivity improvement: keeping careful track of controllable costs, and identifying and eliminating duplications;

7. Security: informing the work group of all security matters, and making spot checks for possible infraction of the security regulations;

8. Coordination with other work units: especially with the units that precede the work of a supervisor's unit, and the one that immediately follows it;

9. Contact with outside and inside customers: dealing with internal customers on a daily basis and external customers when appropriate;

10. Forward planning: being aware of organizational goals and objectives, and developing a working plan to implement the tasks that will move the company in the direction of these goals and objectives;

11. Keeping management informed: communicating upward in the organization is as important as communicating downward;

12. Budgeting: initiating budgeting processes and keeping informed through regular and current updates of financial conditions.

If the list of supervisory duties appears formidable, it is. However, all these duties must be performed. And the best person to assure that everything happens on time, on budget, and as planned is the supervisor, not the manager or staff groups. Should supervisors abandon or delegate these accountabilities, or staff groups usurp them, the organization's structure and performance will be weakened.

Because of the enormity of the job of supervision, organizations are often tempted to off-load some of the supervisory duties to others. Managers will tend to take on parts of the job in a well-meaning effort to relieve the pressure on supervisors. Or interim positions such as lead-workers or assistant supervisors are created. The problem with these approaches is the potential for dilution of accountability.

It has been demonstrated over and over again that improvements must occur at the level that is directly accountable for the results. Shared accountability does not work. Those who preach this concept apparently have not had to live with the consequences of a bad choice. Accountability is a singular concept. When we share accountability, we tend to fail in producing the desired results. And the corrections, if any, are not focused. If we divide the accountability, we must also divide the corrections-a formidable, if not impossible task.

The critical issue for management is to make sure that they are not bypassing or undermining supervision. Supervision is so critical to an organization that, if it does not happen at the right level, it will happen at the managerial level or even at the top management level. In some mismanaged organization it even happens at the staff level.

Consider this scenario. On the golf course, the president of XYZ Company says to his good friend, the president of ABC Company, "Listen, Pete, one piece of business before we tee off. My people tell me that the last batch of widgets you sent us was defective. The holes are too small and the fluids won't pass through. What happened?" Of course, Pete doesn't know the answer but promises to check into it first thing Monday morning.

On Monday, Pete, a strong believer in the chain of command, calls in his vice president of manufacturing. "Jerry, we have a problem with those widgets we sent to XYZ last week. What size hole did you drill in that batch?"

Jerry, having been around the block a few times,

knows how to answer a question from the president when he doesn't know the answer. "I don't know, but I'll find out," and immediately sets off to find his manager of manufacturing.

"Listen, George, that last batch of widgets we sent to XYZ? What size hole did we drill?" George, not being as experienced and articulate as Jerry but with an intuitiveness indicative of executive potential, replies, "Darned if I know, but I'll check it out."

George carries the question to the supervisor who says he'll check with the mission worker who handled the order.

"Three-eighths" said the mission worker. "Three-eighths" said the supervisor to George, starting it up the chain of command. "Three-eighths," George said to Jerry; "Three-eighths," said Jerry to Pete.

"Three-eighths? How the hell come three-eighths?" asked Pete. Echo, echo, echo–back down the chain of command.

"Because the spec book calls for three-eighths for their application," said the mission worker. And back it goes up the chain of command to the president.

"Everyone knows that for years we have built in a ten percent fudge factor when you use the spec book," says Pete. "I don't want any more widgets going to XYZ Company with less than a half inch hole."

"Yes Sir – Sir – Sir," back down the chain of command.

From high up on mahogany row and without once violating the chain of command, the president of ABC Company just made a supervisory decision–one that clearly effected both the methods and results of a mission work activity. It is certainly within his jurisdiction to do so but in the process he runs the risk of (a) undermining the credibility of his subordinate managers and supervisors, (b) failing to instigate any diagnosis of the widget problem (XYZ may be using the wrong fluids), and (c) implementing a major change in the mission work that is more than likely incorrect.

A supervisory task, when performed by higher management, not only can be the cause of more costly and complicated operations but can also weaken the future performance of the supervisor. In this example, if the supervisor doesn't feel accountable for the job problem, more than likely he or she will not feel the need to be concerned (under similar circumstances) for future improvements. What has happened is that the Supervisor now feels that whenever something goes wrong, management will fix it.

Furthermore, the president of ABC unwittingly made three layers of management into little more than messengers. They had no real input. They had no plan to stop the same thing from happening in the future. They weren't even sure if the CEO's correction was accurate. They may again discover that some widgets are not exactly right for another customer. But that customer may not care to act as ABC's quality control function. That customer may simply take his business elsewhere.

SKILL TRANSFERABILITY

Another significant issue concerning supervision is that the unique skills and knowledge of a supervisor are not transferable from one management tier to the next. The skills required of a supervisor are tied specifically the mission work and to the mission of the unit only. For example, if you were an Executive Director of a hospital and had a supervisory vacancy in the neurosurgery unit, you would not appoint a supervisor from the accounting department (no matter how proficient) to become the supervisor in the neurosurgery department. So it's axiomatic that the skills and the knowledge of a supervisor really aren't transferable; they are extremely unique to the position and to the function.

Just imagine if an executive director of a hospital

believed that "supervision is supervision." What if he or she thought that if a supervisor had mastered all the "Seven Habits," all the human relation techniques, and all the generic skills (i.e. planning, directing, and decision-making), and had been trained in diversity management and sexual harassment issues, then a supervisor could supervise any function. Ask any supervisor who has worked in the real world, and they'll say that putting people in supervision that do not know the basics of the work they will supervise is a prescription for disaster.

Non-transferability of supervisory performance creates a certain "level of discontinuity" in the organization. Thus, a supervisor should not be promoted to become a manager based solely on the skills acquired as a supervisor. Supervisors promoted to the manager level must learn a whole new set of skills and knowledge that are completely different from supervisory skills.

THE FULL JOB OF SUPERVISION

The job of supervision as we have described it to this point is indeed a very big one. However, there's more. Rarely does a supervisor's job description contain all that is required of the position, unless you include the infamous line at the bottom that reads, "And all other duties as assigned." There are other duties that most supervisors do not discover until they begin to work in the position.

Let's take a look at a time period–a week, a month, a year–and identify the types of activities in which supervisors are likely to be involved.

1. Mission work. We have yet to work with an organization in which supervisors do not spend some time doing mission work. To some extent this is legitimate in cases of emergency, filling in for vacations, keeping up with skills, and pitching in on occasion when the workload is very heavy. However,

too often supervisors will get involved with the mission work because (A) it's what they're comfortable with, (B) they don't know what to do as a supervisor but they do know the mission work, or (C) the manager places too much pressure on meeting mission work goals and too little pressure on carrying out supervisory duties. Legitimate or not, doing mission work takes critical time from doing supervision.

2. Head of Group (HOG) Tasks. Anyone who is in a box on an organization chart is expected to carry out certain duties that have nothing to do with the work they supervise or manage. These duties include such things as collecting United Way funds, attending award banquets, professional meetings, and representing the company in civic functions or community activities. These are certainly commendable activities but again they do take time away from supervision.

3. Boss Imposed Duties (BIDs). These are duties assigned by supervisors' managers, sometimes for developmental purposes, sometimes because the manager will not be available due to vacation or business trips, and sometimes because the manager just doesn't want to do the project.

4. Fire-fighting. This involves assisting with emergencies in some other part of the organization.

5. "Administrivia." This is a coined word to identify the myriad of administrative duties, mostly requiring lots of paperwork that supervisors have to complete. In many instances, this duty requires an enormous amount of a supervisor's time and, with government regulations and compliance require-

ments ever-increasing, there appears to be no letup in sight.

6. Supervision. Some of the time, supervisors do in fact supervise.

While the amount of time devoted to each of these categories may vary from organization to organization and from supervisor to supervisor, one concept is common to all. The one compressible duty among the seven listed-the only one the supervisor has control over-is supervision. Rarely will a supervise refuse to do any activity or an assignment in the other six categories. For example, if the manager says to the supervisor, "Hey, Charlie, I'll be at the convention for the next week and I need some data for a presentation I have to make when I get back. Would you mind getting it for me while I'm gone?" Rare is the supervisor who would say, "No, sir. It's not my job."

Routine versus Payoff Duties

When Charlie has to collect the data for his boss, from what activity does Charlie steal the time to do so? From the only activity he has control over-supervision. This is one of the reasons supervision has over time become a weaker link in the management chain. There are simply too many non-supervisory activities demanding the time that should be devoted to supervision.

Unfortunately, the problem does not end there. It gets worse. As mentioned in the preceding chapter, within the supervisory category there are two types of duties that supervisors should be performing. One category is called routine duties. These are duties that must be performed. They are system-demanded, process-demanded, or boss-demanded. These are the types of duties that, if not performed, will cause the supervisor to hear about it loud and clear. Typical among them would be daily production reports, hourly machine readings, schedules, task assignments, and time cards.

The other category is called payoff duties. These are duties that do not have to be done-they are not demanded-but if accomplished will produce improvements in some aspect of work. Typically, payoff duties make things better, faster, less costly, or safer. However, unlike routine duties, they can be stymied by procrastination since there is no immediate demand that they be accomplished. Thus, when Charlie collects data for the boss and steals time from supervisory duties to do so, he will most likely put a payoff duty on the back burner.

As mentioned earlier, supervisors are the members of management who are closest to the mission work and thus, along with their mission workers, are in the best position to recognize and implement improvements. Yet, when demands are made in the non-supervisory categories, improvement activities are the first to go. In one of our supervisory workshops, we give the supervisors a complete list of supervisory duties, comprised of both routine and payoff duties. We ask them to go through the list and check the duties they are not performing. Invariably, the ones they check are payoff duties.

Supervisors who are not continuously working on one or more payoff duties at any point in time are not earning their keep. Without payoff improvements being implemented, the best that can be hoped for is maintenance of the status quo. It is more than likely not the supervisor's fault. The problem lies in a total management system that has downgraded and degraded supervision to the point that supervisors are little more than mission workers, data keepers and paper pushers.

We have much more to say on this topic in the next chapter since it is the manager's job to assure that supervisors are doing the full job of supervision. If there are performance problems at any level of the organization, the first place to look is one level up.

When Supervisors Don't Supervise

Make no mistake about it, the mission work will get supervised, regardless of who does it. If supervisors don't supervise, someone will. The most likely candidates would be their bosses, the managers. Once this happens, the entire management structure is pulled down one or more levels. The net result is that managers are now supervising and top management is now managing.

We often hear managers and supervisors whining and complaining about executives micro-managing their projects. To be fair, some executives are micro-managers and just "can't let go." Others, however, including the very best executives among them, will turn to micro-management of projects and critical organizational activities when managers and supervisors are not doing their jobs. Micro-management and its fallout, however, is not the major problem. The real detriment to the organization comes from top management being pulled down into the internal structure to deal with operational issues. This means less or no time being devoted to the external issues that will determine the long-term fate of the organization.

If the top executives are busy running the organization internally, who is going to do the job of the top executives? The answer is not "no one." There are those out there in the business world that can't wait for the day when your top management is no longer visible in the external arena: your competitors. They would love to have a clear path to your major customers, to government agencies and legislators, to all of the sources of influence that make decisions critical to the future of the organization.

It is apparent that the performance of the supervisory level, positive or negative, has ramifications far beyond getting the product out the door. Our hope is that this book, among other things, will begin to restore the respect and enhance the perception of importance that this level of management deserves.

CHAPTER SIX

MANAGING A MULTI-LEVEL ORGANIZATION

For many years in the work we have done with hundreds of middle managers in all types of organizations, we have asked them this question, "How would you describe a successful middle manager?" The answers are predictable since most managers are weaned on a results-at-all-costs philosophy. Thus, the typical answer is, "The successful manager gets the work out, on schedule, within costs and quality parameters and meets all the requirements of safety, policy, and procedures."

There is no question about the legitimacy of the answer since the manager who doesn't get the work out within those parameters certainly won't be a manager very long. However, two things strike us about this response to our question. First, the response describes work that other people do since in most instances it is the mission workers who are accountable for getting the work out. The response says nothing about what a successful manager does as a manager to assure that the work gets out. The results only concept explains why many managers spend a good deal of time actually doing the mission work or directly supervising it rather than allowing supervisors and mission workers to do what they get paid for.

The second problem with the results-only definition of a successful manager is that results are always measured either in real time or ex post facto. There is no inherent demand for on-going improvement of those results or for managerial activities that are future-directed. Thus, the results-only concept implies that a manager can be successful by devoting all his or her time to getting today's work out with little regard for tomorrow.

Our national romance with numbers, measurability,

and computer reports has made management-by-the-numbers a more common definition of success than logic and conventional wisdom would indicate. If you study, as we have for years, the truly outstanding managers, you will see very quickly that numbers and results are only a common denominator, however important they are. Most managers produce results; the great ones go well beyond.

Around 1916, Henri Fayol maintained that managing is a series of functions such as planning, organizing, coordinating, and controlling. Louis Allen designed his popular management seminars in the '60s and early '70s around those functions. As other management functions were discussed, more "ings" were added to the function of a manager such as motivating, scheduling, and a myriad of others. As Henry Mintzberg (Harvard Business Review, July-August, 1975) and others found out, these are not what managers do. Henry Minztberg put to rest some of what he called folklore about managing. For example, he said that it is folklore that a manager "is a reflective, systematic planner." In fact he found out that managers daily activities consist of "brevity, variety, and discontinuity."

We reason that a manager's job is not planning, organizing, coordinating, and controlling, not because a manager does not engage in those activities, but rather those activities are so general that everyone in an organization plans, organizes, coordinates, and controls. The functions are not unique-they are generic and common to most everyone who works in an organization. It makes little sense to define a management position by the functions that that position carries out, particularly when everyone carries out those functions to varying degrees.

Mintzberg concluded his article by writing that: "No job is more vital to our society than that of the manager. It is the manager who determines whether our social institutions serve us well or whether they squander our talents and resources."

We agree with the value Mitzberg has put on the job

of a manager. Yet, throughout the literature on management, the job has been intellectualized beyond its reality. Professors have tried to make managers in their own vision. Academicians do not study and work with large enough successful managers to find out what they really do.

Allen I. Kraut and Patricia R. Pedigo from IBM and D. Douglas McKenna and Marvin D. Dunnette from Personnel Decisions Research Institute, Inc. conducted some very enlightening research. Their findings were published in The Academy of Management publication, Executive (1989, Vol. III, No. 4.) They wrote, "Management, we believe, is a team sport that makes similar demands of its players. Unfortunately, many executives (the 'team captains') and managers do not recognize how managerial jobs are similar and yet different across organizational levels and functions. This lack of mutual understanding among players can make it very difficult for them to appreciate one another's work and coordinate their work activities. It can make winning that much harder."

There has been a lot written about management, but few if any authors have been as succinct and practical as those authors we quoted above. As we will discuss further in the chapter on hierarchy, Kraut, Pedigo, McKenna, and Dunnette recognize that managers must perform both common and unique functions. At each level of management and supervision, there are common skills that every level contributes. But common skills do not define a management level's contribution—it is the skills unique to each level that determines organizational contributions. Common skills merely get today's job completed. In football, for example, common skills such as running, blocking and tackling are not enough to identify who is contributing what to the success of the team. Adding the unique skills of a quarterback, a wide receiver, a center, and others determines the ultimate success of the team.

Researchers Kraut and Pedigo and McKenna completed their studies in 1989; we started ours in 1965 and have continued it to the present time.

LEADERS VERSUS MANAGERS

Managing is a rational act of conducting business to achieve all the stated goals and objectives of a business in an organized way. Chaos and uncertainty are the antithesis of managing. Lately, however, due to the proliferation of some popular, but not practical, books on management, rationality seems to have given way to flimsy theorizing about leaders and managers. Recent publications on the topic do little to clarify or enhance the role of either.

In most of his books (*Visionary Leadership, Leaders Who Make a Difference*) and other writings, Burt Nanus compares the attributes of a manager to those of a leader. Many of his subjects are famous business visionaries. In his writings his tendency is to define the manager as a paper-pusher, an administrator (in the sense of a drudge), a robot with no sense of humanity whose only job is to order others around. Yet the leader, from Nanus' view, is someone with a vision, a creative person who communicates with passion. For instance, he writes: "The manager is a copy; the leader is original….The manager imitates; the leader originates."

It is difficult to give credence to the attributes of a leader as described in these publications since leadership is difficult to define and comes in many shapes and sizes. Identifying the attributes of a leader by studying leaders is inherently biased simply by the author's selection of which leaders to study. A further assumption is that the leader possessing all the attributes-the virtual leader-most likely does not exist. Most known leaders may possess one or more of the attributes but not all of them.

Given Nanus' bent, it comes as no surprise that many of the known leaders in Nanus' analysis were poor managers. Henry Ford is often described as a leader who had a vision of making cars for the masses. Yet Ford had a miserable relationship with his workers, and almost lost the company due to his stubbornness. If a clear vision and the ability to persuasively communicate that vision are attributes of a leader, then Henry Ford qualifies on the former but fails on the latter.

It is ironic that in the volumes of books about leadership, most authors have ignored one of the basic requirements of a leader—a leader must have followers! Actually, followers determine the value of a leader. There has been very little written about "followership." Is it assumed that good "leaders" will overcome problems of their followers? Is followership blind obedience? We think not. Followership is a skill just as important as leadership that must be learned and practiced in order to make a true work team. After all, 80 percent of the accomplishments in an organization are achieved by the followers and only 20 percent by the leaders.

In an interesting exercise, we applied the leadership attributes Nanus summed up and found no leaders, other than Hitler, Stalin, Mao Tse Tung, and others of that ilk, who had most of the attributes. Ironically, the one leader we did find that had all of the attributes of a leader was the person who introduced and marketed the Pet Rock. That's not exactly a resounding endorsement of the so-called attributes of leadership.

Do these statements imply that a manager cannot be a leader? And that a leader would not be an effective manager? Are the two mutually exclusive? Imagine telling a manager, "Look, Mary, you're a manager. You shouldn't be indulging in creative thinking, innovation, and discussing future goals with your people. That's Charlie's job. He's the leader. You just concentrate on getting the routine, administrative stuff done."

This current trend to distinguish managing from leading is empty-minded theorizing. It is a form of stereotyping that can impede the growth and development of management talent and weaken the management structure of an organization. Almost all authors writing on leadership have denigrated and demeaned the role of management. They believe a manager is good only when he or she is a leader with the theoretical attributes of leadership as defined by the authors.

THE WHO AND WHY OF MANAGING

In our hierarchy of knowledge, managers as well as mission workers and supervisors are defined by their relationship to the work (not by their position on the organization chart) and have unique functions to perform.

Having identified supervisors as those who have mission workers reporting to them, we follow the same logic to identify managers. Managers are those people in the organization who have supervisors and/or other managers reporting to them. Given that definition, one unique role of managers becomes immediately evident: getting supervisors to supervise or managers to manage.

A second unique role of managers is running the organization internally on a day-by-day basis, otherwise known as internal management, as we refer to it later in this chapter.

In our seminars, we give managers a case scenario involving either a dispute between two departments headed by managers or a project requiring a joint effort between two or more such departments. The question we ask is, "At the manager level, whose job is it to settle the dispute or coordinate joint efforts?" Often the answer is "The next level up. Kick it upstairs." This is often a reflex response because managers over the years have been conditioned to view their jobs as running their own departments-the traditional pyramid. If that logic is followed, however, the dispute may be taken all the way to top management to resolve. When managers are asked if they want top management spending their time on operational disputes, the immediate answer is, "No. Plus we don't want top management micro-managing our departments." When asked, "Who then should have handled the dispute in the first place?" they are forced to admit it is the managers of the respective departments.

Dealing with interdepartmental activities-lateral coordination-is a direct responsibility of managers. "Kicking things upstairs" should occur only when the respective managers are first unable to resolve a dispute or agree upon a course of action.

In addition to accountability for lateral coordination, managers do have vertical accountability for their pyramids-that is, accountability for the activities and functions of those people and operating units that report to them. If you then combine lateral and vertical accountabilities – both across and down the organization chart-it becomes apparent that the range of these accountabilities forms a hexagon, with managers at the top and encompassing all the activities and units below them. Within the hexagon, supervisors and mission workers are also expected to function both laterally and vertically. Thus, the day-to-day operations of the organization occur through the collective and combined efforts of all within the hexagon, directed by the managers at the top. In our Hierarchy of Knowledge, special knowledge and expertise is required of middle managers to carry out the unique accountability for internal management.

MANAGING WORK AND MANAGING THE ORGANIZATION

Managing encompasses two major areas: managing work and managing multiple levels within an organization. By definition, managers oversee the mission worker level, the supervisory level, and in large organizations, often other management levels. If managers do not run and advise multiple levels within their departments, they are not managers. They may be called managers by title, but by substance they are either supervisors or mission workers. By definition, if they only have one level below them, they are supervisors, regardless of title (manager, director, or vice president). If they don't even have one level, they are mission workers, again regardless of title.

Managing Work

Managers are concerned with providing resources so that the work of the organization can be accomplished. Functions performed often include the following:

> 1. Budgeting. This process is basically an attempt to predict the needed resources for a designated project and identify how much and in what category these resources will be allotted so the work units can accomplish their tasks.

> 2. Planning. This function is a rational organizing of events to clarify how the designated budget should be spent, and in what sequence.

> 3. Organizing. This task provides for the establishment of logical work units to implement plans made according to the budget allocation.

Although we agree with Henri Fayol and Louis Allen that the "ings" are critical parts of a manager's job, to define the job entirely in those terms is both simplistic and misleading. Historically, budgeting, planning, and organizing work have been basic topics in a manager's early on-the-job training. Obviously, every manager must perform these "survival" functions. However, the job of managing must provide more than the ability to just survive. Managers must be accountable for the growth and improvement of performance in their respective areas. That is why they must be able to perform well in the second major area of their job, which is not often practiced well-managing a multi-level organization.

Organizational Weaknesses

The greatest weaknesses of the organizations we have observed and worked with have been in the area of top management in multi-level organizations. We believe the most significant questions to be answered by top management are these: What are the issues unique to this particular business and who should be accountable to perform tasks specific to those issues and be equipped with the unique knowledge and skills to do so?

To answer the second question first, we strongly believe that middle managers must perform the tasks. Top executives should not be involved with the business' daily functions relating to internal management. If top executives do become involved, their own function (external management) will suffer.

If one level of middle managers does not acquire the appropriate unique skills and practice them, the organization often creates several additional layers of middle management to compensate. Too many management levels create a bureaucratic hierarchy instead of a "knowledge hierarchy." Massive layoffs of managers (as occurred in the '80s) are the price paid for creating excessive levels of middle managers.

Using and practicing the knowledge hierarchy requires fewer levels of management to run an organization effectively. It allows middle managers, through their specific and unique knowledge, to truly manage the multi-level organization, as opposed to working with bits and pieces of knowledge scattered among several levels of management. The powerful and unique knowledge for managers is not inherent in the mission work, but is rather in the skills of managing a multi-level organization.

There are three major components to middle management's work: getting the supervisors to supervise, organization management, and opportunity management.

Getting the Supervisors to Supervise

Those managers who are able to get their supervisors to perform the full job of supervision are way ahead of the rest. It is not an easy process, even though the statement sounds simple. There are as many issues that managers should avoid, as there are activities that they must perform. Managers must make sure that they do not usurp the functions belonging to their supervisors. Supervisory tasks, by their nature, are urgent. This urgency too often causes managers to jump in and take control, which, as we've stated previously, causes two problems. It prevents supervisors from doing their job, unwittingly training them to abdicate their responsibilities and to depend on the managers to step in when problems occur. It also steals time from supervisors performing their own functions adequately and successfully.

The job of supervision is so crucial in the organization that it requires a strong discipline from managers not to perform it, but to make sure that it is done in a timely fashion by their supervisors.

Implied in the manager's accountability for getting supervisors to supervise is the on-going training and development of the supervisors. Unfortunately, in most instances the process of training and development gets off to a very slow start.

More often than not new supervisors are informed of their promotion on a Friday afternoon. When does their new job begin? On Monday, of course, as though something magical happens over the weekend to transform them from mission workers into supervisors. They learn to survive by trial and error and by doing what other supervisors do. Whatever formal training they receive is limited to the infamous "ings" mentioned earlier in this chapter. Thus, they learn the "hows" of supervision but rarely do they learn the "whats."

It is amazing to us how few supervisors are ever told what they are accountable for beyond getting the work out. In training, they learn that their mission workers should have a clear understanding of their responsibilities and the standards to which they are to perform. Yet, the supervisors themselves are rarely given the same information about their jobs.

George Ordiorne, the father of Management by Objectives (MBO), identified the first step in the MBO process to be the mutual agreement between supervisors and managers as to the specific duties of the supervisor. Objectives and performance plans for the supervisors were then created. Following the initial success of MBO, Ordiorne admitted that much of the improvement in supervisory performance thought to be the result of setting objectives was in fact due to a clear understanding of job duties. "For the first time," said many supervisors, "I know what's expected of me."

In the studies Ordiorne conducted in deriving the MBO concept, he found that on the average managers and their subordinate supervisors agree on only about 70 percent of what the supervisors' duties should be. That means that they disagree on about 30 percent of the supervisors' duties. Disagreement in this instance means that both the managers and supervisors had items on their list that the other did not have. Not only is 30 percent a significant difference but also the disagreements tended to be related to payoff duties. In other words, they agreed on the routine duties-those things that had to be done-but disagreed on those duties that would cause process and performance improvements.

Eliminating that 30 percent difference has the potential for immediately improving supervisory performance and would reinforce the critical importance of allowing payoff duties to compete successfully with routine duties in terms of priorities and resources.

Will the 30 percent disagreement ever be completely eliminated? Probably not, according to Ordiorne. He illustrates this point by relating an incident that occurred while he was working with a client organization. His process was to ask the manager to list the duties that the manager felt his supervisors should be performing. Ordiorne would then go to that manager's supervisors and ask them to do the same. Then Ordiorne would compare the lists and report the results back to the manager. In this instance he had collected the manager's list and those of four or five of the manager's supervisors.

When Ordiorne went to supervisor #5 to pick up his list, the supervisor said, "George, I have the list ready, but, before I give it to you, would it be worth ten dollars for you to show me the list my boss prepared for me?"

"You can't buy the integrity of a university professor for ten bucks," said Ordiorne, "but, if you'll give me the price of a cup of coffee, I won't have to know that you pulled this page out of my folder, copied it, and put the original back."

A month later, when Ordiorne returned to present his findings to the manager, the manager said, "George, am I glad to see you. Sit down. We've got to talk. I don't know what you did to supervisor number five, but his performance for the past thirty days has been spectacular. It's almost as though he could read my mind. Tell me, George, did you show supervisor number five the list I had prepared for him?"

"I can't lie to you," replied George, "Yes, I did."

"I knew it," said the manager, "that SOB cheated."

Managers apparently don't want supervisors to know everything. So 100 percent agreement may not be realistic, but 98 to 99 percent is a real possibility.

Our company, Practical Management Inc., has for many years utilized an approach to developing supervisors that is simply called "The Process." Effective managers work with their supervisors in the twelve unique areas we have identified in Chapter Five on Supervision. All twelve areas might not apply to every organization, but managers must review them, and work closely with supervisors to meet the objectives set in each applicable section.

In working with The Process, the first step is for the managers to meet with their supervisors and to review the twelve broad areas of supervisory accountability. After the review, the supervisors should be asked to identify at least three activities in each broad area that they feel they should be but are not now performing. The actual decision and listing of activities should be done individually by each supervisor.

Managers should allow about two weeks for the supervisors to complete the task. During that two-week period, managers should make similar lists, defining what their expectations are for their supervisors in each category.

Then, in a meeting with the supervisors, the manager should facilitate a process of merging the two lists, a task requiring detailed discussions and some negotiations. This first step in The Process takes time and should not be rushed, even if two or more meetings are required. The result of these meeting will be a merged list of what both the manager and the supervisors agree are critical tasks.

In the second stage of The Process, the manager should ask the supervisors to concentrate their efforts during the next two months in the critical tasks agreed upon. In addition, the supervisors should document the obstacles that prevent them from performing the agreed upon tasks at the highest level. After a two-month trial, the manager should meet with supervisors and review the results of their performance, as well as review the list of the obstacles the supervisors have identified.

Most often, the obstacles will be in two areas: organizational and individual. The organizational obstacles must be discussed fully with the supervisors in order to create agreed-upon plans to remove the obstacles (or at least to reduce their negative impact.) As a part of the plans, managers should be ready to commit to working with their peer managers, heads of other units, or their bosses to assist in obstacle removal. Until the organizational obstacles are removed, the expectations of performance from the supervisors in the problem areas should be minimal.

Individual performance obstacles are often due to lack of training or know-how. Most performance obstacles can be discussed within the group to discover how other supervisors have overcome the obstacles. This could well be a good peer training session. If the obstacles are due to lack of training, an immediate plan should be devised in which supervisors can obtain the necessary skills.

This process must be reviewed and adjusted yearly. Managers must look at the resources needed for each objective, and work on a plan to obtain them. It is an obvious waste of time to meet with supervisors, have them work on various tasks, but provide no resources to achieve them. If no resources to achieve changes can be provided, the expectation for improvement must be reduced or eliminated.

This job of managers-getting supervisors to supervise-is so critical that without achieving success in this function, other managerial tasks become irrelevant. Once supervisors have a clear understanding of their accountability and have been trained in basic supervisory techniques, on-going development under the guidance of the manager becomes critical.

A powerful technique that we call the "fifteen-second pause" can assist managers in the on-going development of their supervisors. The technique requires managers to pause for fifteen seconds before rushing into crisis situations or when making critical decisions. They then ask themselves this question: "How can I get what I want (a problem handled, a critical project completed) and, at the same time, make my supervisors stronger in performing similar activities in the future?" Rather than handling the situation themselves, managers should first consider how they could help the supervisor handle it in a way that the supervisor becomes stronger in dealing with those kinds of issues. This is true supervisory development because it occurs in real time, during the heat of battle, and in the day-to-day operating environment.

A manager in an organization we worked with conducted an attitude survey among the mission workers in her division. Two items from the survey came immediately to her attention. One was that mission workers perceived their supervisors as being poor communicators. To deal with that problem she promptly sent them to a training session on communications. The other survey result indicated poor morale stemming from a perception that the company was in financial trouble and considering layoffs. The manager knew the rumors were untrue; the company was doing well and there had been no talk about layoffs. To lay the rumors to rest she called an all hands meeting and informed everyone about the true financial status.

Her method of squelching the rumors has a direct bearing on the supervisors being perceived as poor communicators. She is what is known as a "good news manager." If there's good news to give, she gives it; if there is bad news, the supervisors deliver it.

Had she taken the "fifteen-second pause" before the all-hands meeting she could have asked herself how she could stop the rumors and develop her supervisors as good communicators in the eyes of their mission workers, she would have taken an entirely different approach. This might have meant giving the information to the supervisors first and having them communicate it to their mission workers. Or she might have briefed the supervisors first, have them "on stage" with her, and then ended her brief presentation with, "Your supervisors have copies of the current financial data and will discuss the details with you in separate meetings."

Teaching the fifteen-second pause in coaching, mentoring, and training sessions provides a powerful package for the continual development of supervisors, thereby strengthening the entire organization.

Organization Management

The very existence of the manager in a business implies a multi-level organization. A multi-level organization is analogous to the internal combustion engine. Left alone, even if given an inexhaustible supply of everything it needs to run, it will not run indefinitely. It will require preventive maintenance.

Similarly, left alone, a multi-level organization will not operate indefinitely, even if there is an inexhaustible supply of the necessary resources. Just like the engine, if managers do not carry out preventive maintenance on a regular basis, the organization will fail at predictable points.

We have identified seven predictable failure points that are common in multi-level organizations.

Failure Point One
"A multi-level organization, left to itself, will tend to become more costly to operate and less profitable."

Processes, left alone in a multi-level organization, tend to become more elaborate and complex as time goes on. Everyone adds "enhancements" which tend to increase cost without a concomitant increase in profit or effectiveness. Staff people are often the culprits. For example, an auditor may find the petty cash in one area short $50.00. In order to prevent this from happening again, the auditor implements a control system that may cost more than $30,000 a year to operate. This control system clearly adds to the cost of operation without a corresponding benefit. The proliferation of computers, along with the gross overuse of the Internet, E-mail, and voice mail are additional examples of uncontrolled processes going astray.

Prior to Xerox Corporation's change of management, it took more than six months to get approval to change the intensity of a bulb in their duplicating machine required by a customer in Egypt. Why? One reason is that it took almost 100 signatures to get the change started. Further controls delayed the product and added to the cost. Of course the customer couldn't wait that long and purchased the product from a Japanese competitor, who implemented the changes needed overnight.

Failure Point Number Two
"A multi-level organization, left to itself, will not operate as designed to operate."

Any process in an organization goes through changes. Some changes may improve the original product or service. But others are made without any thought given to the consequences.

We were told of a humorous example of this phenomenon that happened in the Marquard Corporation. Some engineers, in search of efficiency, studied the use of paper towels in the company bathrooms. They determined that the kind of towel dispensers they used wasted too many paper towels, because in pulling down one paper towel several of them fell out and were wasted. Their calculation showed that the company was wasting $8,000 a year in paper towels. They recommended that the dispensers be replaced with the kind that you have to crank. They also indicated that cranking the lever is boring and causes the user to stop at the minimum amount of towel. This seemingly logical study resulted in all the towel dispensers being changed

After a few months, another group of engineers studied the amount of time the highly paid engineers must spend in cranking the handle of the new paper towel dispensers. They determined that the loss of time was worth

$40,000 a year. They recommended changing the dispensers. The kind they recommended were the same ones they had before, which allowed precut towels to be pulled out without wasting time cranking. Fortunately the Maintenance Department had not trashed the old ones. They reinstalled them and received the Department-of-the-Month Award for saving the company so much money!

Failure Point Three:
"A multi-level organization, left to itself, will tend to move toward obvious and apparent objectives."

A group of programmers, left to themselves, will create programs because that is the obvious and apparent objective for programmers. The question is what contributions do the programs make to the organization? Programs to generate interactive greeting cards or for beating the odds on slot machines may be interesting challenges but create nothing but extra expense to the organization.

Unfortunately, this phenomenon happens too often. Service and staff groups create projects in their specialized areas to be carried out by line people even if the results only benefit the staff group that generated the project. Many training programs are carried out because it is obvious and apparent that the trainer's role is to train even if the training has little relevance to those who receive it.

If a group of people is not too clear as to what the real objective of the greater organization is, they will soon create an objective of their own. Often the objectives decided by the group (but not the organization) tend to reflect what the title of the group is; programmers write programs, controllers control, auditors audit, and so on, often without any consideration for the specific needs of the organization. If we're not careful libraries will be designed for librarians, schools for teachers and buildings for architects.

Failure Point Number Four
"A multi-level organization, left to itself, will remove supervisors from the chain of communication."

In multi-level organizations the important news and policies are disseminated through various means: house newsletters, paycheck stuffers, faxes, and E-mails among others. Certainly these instruments have value in disseminating general company information. However, because all employees receive copies, the temptation is to include new policies and other operational information that should be communicated by supervisors. Conventional wisdom, verified by management theorists, holds that managers should not by-pass their supervisors. Likewise, written documents should not by-pass their supervisors.

A few years ago Aetna Insurance (then Aetna Life & Casualty) came up with the Performance Bonus Plan designed to pay immediate one-time cash awards to employees chosen for exceptional performance. It was decided that the best way to reach all the employees was to disseminate the plan in the employees' pay envelopes. The problem was the mission workers were paid weekly, their supervisors monthly. The "stuffer" was sent out in one of the weekly pay periods not coinciding with the supervisors' pay.

Add to the problem the fact that the plan was written in a question-and-answer format. One question read, "What do I have to do to get a bonus?" The answer was, "Your supervisor is responsible for determining what accomplishments will be rewarded by bonuses in your area." The final statement in the plan was, "If you have any questions, ask your supervisors." Mission workers were lined up at the supervisor's door before the supervisors had any knowledge of the plan. The supervisors were both embarrassed and angry. What miseries befall supervisors and mission workers in the name of management efficiency!

Also, in the name of efficiency, many organizations

hold all hands meetings so that everyone hears "the news" from the boss at the same time. Managers and supervisors have no chance to digest the material and understand what is happening. In addition, supervisors are hardly perceived as legitimate members of management when they are hearing important news at the same time as their mission workers. This causes both managers and supervisors to lose credibility among their people.

Failure Point Number Five
" A multi-level organization, left to itself, will not develop strategies to meet tomorrow's needs."

Multi-level organizations tend to be image builders and, having built a successful image, to sit on their laurels. They rely on what they have been in the past instead of looking toward tomorrow.

A good analogy of this failure point is when a management vacancy occurs and the organization has to go outside to find the right person, having rejected several current employees for not quite meeting the position specifications. Some time later, the same or similar position becomes available again and the same internal candidates again are rejected.

What happened to the concept of developing people for future positions? To preparing people for promotion? This situation is solid evidence that the organization has not prepared itself to meet the needs of tomorrow.

Failure Point Number Six
"A multi-level organization, left to itself will create and then defend 'deadwood'"

This failure point is a serious indictment of some management practices. Deadwood is defined as a noncontributing employee who has obsolete skills or is somehow not allowed by the organization to use the skills he or she has. Often the deadwood is created by the organization by promoting people above their abilities and not developing employees beyond narrow specialties. For example, often older, more experienced employees are assigned to work on technology that is soon to be phased out while the new hires are working with the replacement technology. When the new technology takes over, the older employees often become deadwood.

Government employees are a good example of this phenomenon. The government hires the employees but often prevents them from performing to their ability because of bureaucratic processes, inept management, and political considerations. The tendency is for the employees to become so discouraged that they give up trying to do their jobs well and simply count the days until they can retire with substantial pensions.

Having caused the deadwood, organizations tend to protect and defend it. They find busy work for the deadwood, kick them upstairs, or give them a backroom job well below their capabilities. The deadwood is defended out of a sense of organization guilt, particularly with loyal, long-term employees, or simply because no self-respecting manager wants to admit to having deadwood.

Failure Point Seven
"A multi-level organization, left to itself, will create roadblocks to supervision."

A staff group in a large moving company decided that, in the name of efficiency, the crews on the trucks needed to be cross-trained. Cross training in this instance meant that the members of the moving crew could do each other's jobs. The furniture movers could pack the china and the packers could move the furniture. The group was successful in selling management on the idea and the orders went out. Conceptually it was no problem, since the techniques for packing and moving the furniture were fairly routine.

The problem developed when the supervisors tried to implement the change without the proper preparation. Because the crews were paid through a system of mileage moved, the faster they got where they were going, the more money they made. Supervisors were also evaluated, in part, on ton mileage moved. Unwisely, no provisions were made in the cross-training plan for the time involved in cross training and the effects of the learning curve on the performance of the crews as well as the supervisors.

This particular obstacle to supervision is what we call a performance conflict. Contradictory demands are placed on the supervisors, neither of which can be accomplished without ignoring or diminishing the other. Call center supervisors are often evaluated on the number of calls per hour made by their reps and the quality of the calls. Good quality calls often take more time than poor ones and thus negatively affect the calls made per hour ratio.

A bank in Alabama instituted a program of cross selling by their tellers. A variety of rewards and prizes were to be awarded for the teller who successfully sold another bank service to a customer. At the same time, another program was started in which customers were to be paid $5 if they stood in the teller line more than five minutes. Do you see the performance conflict for the supervisors who are accountable for the success of both programs?

Obstacles to supervision can occur in any number of other ways. During a sales training program in a pharmaceutical company, sales reps were taught the company's existing sales strategy. Later in the same training program, an outside sales consultant was brought in to teach them an entirely different approach, emphasizing that the traditional approach was no longer effective in today's medical environment. Who was left out of the loop? The supervisors. Being unaware of the consultant's sales strategy, their attempts to coach the new hires on the traditional sales strategy not only fell on deaf ears, but also were openly ridiculed. So much for the influential image of the supervisor.

Successful organization management requires that managers be aware of the failure points of multi-level organizations and take steps to prevent them from happening. Knowing the failure points and preventing them is every bit as important in building an organization as it is with building an automobile engine. "Pay me now, or pay me later" applies equally well to organizations. Once these failure points occur, the cost to fix them can be enormous.

Unfortunately, the failure points and preventive maintenance measures needed by an organization are not as predictable time-wise as in an automobile. Managers must be continually monitoring their organizations to identify beforehand the situations that could produce a failure point and then act to prevent it. This is what we call the art of management since so much of organization management is situational and often involves a specific set of circumstances that may occur in one department but not in others. In addition, preventive measures may involve the lesser of two evils or a "damned if you do and damned if you don't" predicament. For example, how can you have an open-door policy without undermining or encouraging end-runs around your supervisors? Successful managers know that tough decisions have to be made and that they're not going to be right all the time. Nowhere is that more true than with organization management issues.

Opportunity Management

Opportunity management is a search for effectiveness. It is the idea of doing the right things rather than just doing things right. Organizations in their search for efficiency often forget that that which is more efficient may not even be needed. There is no sense in being efficient in processes and work activities that are not making an organizational contribution. Every organizational activity is a candidate for further improvement, but first must pass the contribution test to find out if it is needed at all.

The concept of contributing activities was first recognized by Peter Drucker. Pareto's 80/20 concept, as applied to business, indicates that about 20 percent of the resources or work activities of a corporation produce 80 percent of the results. Drucker maintains that in most organizations the ratio is closer to 90/10 as related to resource utilization. That is, about 10 percent of the resources, or work activities, produce 90 percent of the results. The flip side, of course, is that 90 percent of the activities contribute only 10 percent of the results. Therefore, he reasoned, most activities are questionable in terms of producing results. It is not, however, easy to discover just which activities contribute to the organization and which activities are wasting resources. Being busy is neither an indication of relevancy nor of contribution.

One of the ways to determine whether or not an activity is contributing is to apply the following definition to each activity that utilizes resources: an activity contributes when the result (or the output) of that activity helps satisfy the real need of another segment of the organization. This definition of a contributing activity provides a context within which to evaluate tasks and activities in every unit headed by a manager.

When Dave Staples, one of the founders of Practical Management Inc., worked in the financial department of a large aerospace company, his boss told Dave that he wanted him to go to the various departments and find out if they use a business form called the Monthly Activity and Commitment Report. This was a large, bulky computer run that basically matched expenditures with future commitments.

Dave first approached the manager of Facilities Engineering and asked if he used the Monthly Activity and Commitment Report. When Dave saw a puzzled look on the face of the department manager, he explained the report by indicating its ample size. The department manager recognized it instantly and said, "Oh, you mean the fifty pounder." Sure we use it and find it very useful." When Dave asked how he used the report, the manager indicated it would be easier to show him rather than trying to explain it. He took Dave to a storeroom where there were a number of tables piled high with large blue prints. On each pile there were fifty pounders, one on each corner and one in the middle. "We used to use bricks," said the manager, "but the red stuff got all over the blueprints."

In the definition of a contributing activity we mentioned a real need, not just a perceived need. Certainly the monthly report was meeting a need for the department manager but not the real need for which the report was intended.

In the Field Engineering department of the same corporation, the manager recognized the report immediately. He used the report by cutting out two columns from two different pages, and copied and distributed them to the field engineers. The real need was being met but only by two ounces of the fifty pounds.

Our approach to determining if a task or activity makes a real contribution is called a Needs/Return Analysis. It is based on the concept that feedback determines whether or not the result of the activity is meeting the needs of the user. If there is no feedback, the activity is questionable as to its value. Routine reports that managers and supervisors spend hours completing may simply end up in a file cabinet with no action taken on them and no feedback to the provider to indicate if the reports are even being read.

Managers may well find that an analysis of their own activities and those of their supervisors would uncover any number of noncontributing activities. Eliminating or reducing resource allocations to those activities would free up those resources for application to more productive tasks.

Another technique we use is called the Objectives/Realization. This approach deals with objectives, either organizational or individual, and their potential for being realized. Very often objectives get misinterpreted, misunderstood, convoluted, or changed so dramatically that the original objectives get lost in the process. Our Objectives/Realization ensures that over time the objectives and the activities put in place to meet them are continually monitored. Often changing business conditions and market factors alter the course of an organization, rendering the original objectives either obsolete or of lesser value. If objectives are not modified accordingly, significant resources will be wasted in pursuit of invalid objectives or, more commonly, by costs that outweigh the benefits of fulfilling those objectives.

The Case of the A. J. Rawlins Company

The best way to illustrate the concepts of opportunity management is to relate a case problem, designed by Frank Hoffman, entitled, The A. J. Rawlins Case.

The A. J. Rawlins Company designs, produces, and sells a distinctive line of hydraulic and pneumatic pumps and other fluid type devices. The company employs about 3,500 people, most of whom work at the central headquarters in Brunswick, Ohio. The Brunswick facility is responsible for the company's pump line while two other small plants are engaged in research and the production of highly specialized fluid controls.

All responsibility for sales rests with the individual product department managers, each of whom has their own sales group, headed by a sales manager. The functions of Corporate Marketing are market research, distribution development, market surveys, and new product planning.

Martin Fairlane, sales manager for the Hydraulic Pumps Products Department, has about thirty sales people in the field. A field sales supervisor in each of the five sales areas throughout the country supervises these sales people.

About a year ago, Fairlane decided he could increase sales by bringing one of his best sales people back to the home office to help in up-grading, developing, and training the sales force. Don Stans was the choice. Stans was assigned the job of analyzing the reports of the other sales people and making recommendations to increase their sales. Fairlane gave Stans a completely free hand in recommending improvements, with the only restriction being that they must go out over Fairlane's signature.

From the first reports he reviewed, Stans felt the need for a sales manual as a guide for salespeople. He therefore developed one, based upon his own experience as one of the company's top salespersons. It was a complete volume covering methods of approaching customers, writing up orders, helping customers solve applications problems, and even handling problem customers. The guide took five months to complete. It was issued to all sales people in the field. The sales supervisors were instructed by a letter over Fairlane's signature to require the salespeople to carry the manual with them at all times. Fairlane was ecstatic over the manual and sent one to the Division VP who complimented both Fairlane and Stans by memo.

Four months after issuance of the Sales Manual, Don Stans was in the field on other business and noticed that only one of the eleven sales people he contacted was using the manual and only five of them even knew where their manuals were. He checked with the field supervisor and was told, "I told them to use it, just like it said in Fairlane's memo. But I suspect that the rapid market changes put the material out of date pretty fast. And to be honest with you, I've been so busy keeping Fairlane supplied with 'strategy suggestions and enhancement inputs' that I haven't really checked to see how they use the manual when they contact a customer."

On Stans' recommendation, Fairlane then authorized Stans to select two good salespeople to help keep the manual up to date and to devise a system to guarantee its use. Three more months went into the updating of the manual, much of the time in the field, drawing information from the salespeople and supervisors.

Finally, a system for continuous revision of the Sales Manual, based on "change-notices" from the salespeople, was devised. In addition, sales people were required to initial a report to their supervisor every week, showing how often they had referred to the manual.

The new system was kicked off at the semi-annual meeting by issuing the updated manual to all salespeople. Fairlane proclaimed that the manual was the key to sales success during the near-term period until his long-range strategy concepts could be understood and accepted by other members of management. He again complimented Stans for the significant contributions he was making with the manual.

Stans and his two assistants then turned to the writing of sales plans while awaiting the first "change-notices" from the field. They soon discovered several approaches to stimulating higher sales in the field. Stans called Fairlane's secretary for an appointment and was put on the list. But Fairlane was busy and it was four days before he could talk to Stans. When he did, he was interested but was so involved in a long-range strategy development with the research people that he could not follow through. Fairlane asked Stans to take the plan around the field and get the sales supervisors' reactions to it.

While making the rounds over the next two months, Stans found supervisors generally unreceptive to his proposed sales-stimulation approaches. The supervisors were defensive about the way they currently apportioned salespeople's territories, critical of the disruption the new approaches would cause in salespeople's routine and morale, and tactfully hostile toward Stans' role in "telling them how to run their field offices." Stans gained little support for the new approaches, although in his heart he knew he was right.

Incidentally, during these same rounds, the supervisors complimented him on the improved sales manual. They said it was much clearer and more thorough than the previous one and was the most complete sales reference they had ever had. After telling Stans this, two of them even put it in writing in memos to Fairlane. Stans was pleased that the manuals were at last successful.

Stans prepared some recommendations based upon his findings:

1. Institute the new sales-stimulation approaches;

2. Rotate the sales supervisors, so they will not feel the new approaches are threatening reflections upon their handling of their current assignments; and,

3. Put two more people (preferably two of the better sales supervisors) on the "manual task force team" to go around to each sales person and follow-up right on the spot to make sure the manuals get used to even greater advantage.

He took this report to Fairlane who said, "Good, good, I'm glad you got the thinking of the field people. I'm sure your report will be helpful. I'll get to it as soon as I can. Right now though I am getting ready for a sales strategy meeting with the product engineer and the department manager. I'm going to get 'em to really see the importance of strategic-thinking this time, when I spring my analysis of the impact of our products on space travel."

This case study includes the following questions:

1. As a part of a cost reduction program, the president set up a Manpower Analysis Team to go to each department to determine how effectively resources, particularly manpower, were being used. In responding to the Manpower Analysis Team, how is Fairlane going to justify Stans' job?

Fairlane has to justify Stans' job by indicating that Stan's job is to increase sales. If Fairlane is asked by the manpower team what Stans does to increase sales, Fairlane must say he writes and up-dates sales manuals. In this case what Stans does and what he contributes are two different things. Activity does not mean contribution. A contribution is made only when the activity's output produces the desired results, in this case increased sales. Yet, there is no indication that Stans' efforts are helping to increase sales.

2. What questions should Fairlane have asked to find out if the manual was the key to increased sales?

He should have asked: "Are the salespeople using the manuals? Have the sales increased? Is the increase due to the use of manuals? Without answering these questions, there is no way to tell if the manuals were successful after all. Yet Fairlane utilized the time of the three best sales people, taking them out of a revenue-producing unit and putting them on "the manual task force," a non-revenue producing unit with questionable value as a contributing activity.

3. Let's make some assumptions: let's say we have determined that by using the manual salespeople can increase their sales. Assume this as a fact. Making it quantifiable, let's say that the nine salespeople who have used the manual have increased their sales by 30 percent, whereas the sales of the other twenty-one sales people have remained the same. Therefore, it is to our benefit to get the other twenty-one sales people to use the manual and obtain a similar result. Would this justify Stans' request of adding two more people to the "manual task force team" to get the other twenty-one salespeople to use the manual?

Those who answer, "Yes, the pay-off is significant if twenty-one salespeople can increase sales by thirty percent," are confusing Opportunity Management with opportunism. In managing an organization, benefits must be judged by the right structure-that is, the right people doing the right things, and not just by the immediate, short-term results. The "manuals team" is a staff group that if it is to have any organizational value should be serving the sales department in an advisory function. The team may well assist in designing and promoting the manual. However, in place already are the right people to ensure the use of the manual-the sales supervisors.

There are times when Opportunity Management requires experimentation. The purpose of experimentation, however, should be to increase the return for the costs incurred. Cost-benefit analyses should be ongoing to identify the point at which the costs outweigh the potential benefits. Peter Drucker is quick to point out that the 90/10 concept occurs in large part because of the tendency of managers to solve problems rather than to seize opportunities.

In the A. J. Rawlins Company there was a clear misapplication of resources. Clearly Martin Fairlane was not managing sales nor was he working directly with his sales supervisors. Rather, in his efforts to promote long-term sales strategies, he was trying to do the job of Corporate Marketing.

The significance of opportunity management is to discover the contributing activities and put resources where the organizational pay off is rather than chasing the rainbow for immediate and short lived "opportunism."

WHY MANAGERS FAIL

When managers fail to reach their potential in an organization the failure is almost never due to lack of education or training. It is the organization that causes a manager to fail.

A managerial failure usually occurs at one of three times: at the time the manager is selected, during the developmental stage, and at the managerial maturity stage.

The failure most often occurs during the selection stage. The tendency is for the criteria used to reflect the currently popular leadership characteristics, those with vision who can see the "big picture" and do not get bogged down in details. Yet, the nature of mission work and supervision is to be concerned with details, to be sure quality products and services get delivered on time. The very traits that make workers good at their lower level jobs may well preclude them from being promoted into supervision and subsequently into managing. Thus, the characteristics that are often used to exclude a person from being selected as a manager are traits that may in fact enable that person to become an effective manager.

In discussing the hierarchy of knowledge, we indicated that each level in an organization requires different skills and knowledge. If one level were the extension of the previous level, we would end up with a great deal of duplication and additional levels of management. Management would be better served by first identifying the demands and accountabilities of specific management levels and then creating a pool of candidates who are best capable of learning the new skills and knowledge in the shortest period of time.

Failure at the developmental stage occurs when the individual does not recognize the levels of discontinuity and keeps using the same skills and knowledge that brought success in the previous position. Outstanding skills in mission work are excellent qualifications for supervision, but those skills have only limited value in becoming an effective supervisor. The same concept applies to a manager who has moved up from the ranks of supervision.

A complete change of skills must either be communicated to the individual by the organization and appropriate training be provided, or the individual must recognize it and take steps to acquire and implement the new skills. Otherwise the person will be bound to fail as a manager. The failure will not be caused by the lack of education or ability but by the organization's failure to identify the new and unique demands of the position and to provide the new managers with the necessary training and development.

At the maturity stage four talent killers can cause organizational failures:

1. Not providing the appropriate supervisory or management training programs. Or offering the training, but not demanding the skills learned to be used on the job. To cause the newly developed skills to be used on the job requires monitoring, follow up, and coaching by higher management until the newly acquired skills become comfortable to perform.

2. Promoting too quickly. When promotions to a new management level occur too quickly, there is inadequate time for the person to learn the unique skills demanded at the previous level. Premature promotions cause failure due to a person's inability to master the specific skills in one level before moving to the next level.

It is an interesting phenomenon that although a successful person does not use the skills of the lower hierarchy, that person must be very familiar with them. Simply stated, one must have detailed knowledge of the level below and the unique skills for the current level. The knowledge of the previous level provides for effective execution of the new skills as well as a basis for coaching others. Pooled ignorance is often the result when neither the coach nor the coachee is experienced in the skills being taught.

Without the ability to coach others, managers cannot achieve optimal results from their work units. The result can be a talent killer since not only does the new manager fail but also upper management loses confidence in his or her ability to be upwardly mobile.

3. Insufficient rewards for the proper performance, or rewards for the wrong performance, is another talent killer. For example, when a sales manager is rewarded for personally selling a big contract, the temptation will be to continue to make more personal sales. Add that to the fact that new managers are more comfortable selling than they are managing, and soon they are spending more time with prospects than they are with their sales supervisors.

People should be rewarded for the work they are accountable for performing-managers for managing, supervisors for supervising, and mission workers for the mission work. Too often, the incentives for management are directly related to the performance of their subordinates. Bonuses paid to managers because their departments met or exceeded performance goals are rewards for successful performance of the mission work. It doesn't take long for managers to realize that the more time they spend doing mission work or supervising it, the greater the rewards. In addition, managers whose departments meet operational goals are more likely to be promoted.

Not only is this incentive process more costly to the organization, the real price is more devastating. Managers who do not manage are abdicating their responsibilities to their supervisors and mission workers. The development of potential at those levels is neglected and a source of major talent is lost to the organization. Good people are good, in part, because they seek to grow in their jobs and to be prepared for greater responsibility. If their drive to improve in their jobs is not satisfied that drive will either dissipate or the person will go to work elsewhere.

WHAT GREAT MANAGERS KNOW

From our years of working with middle managers, we have discovered that the great ones know and do several things that the others do not.

They know exactly what managing is.

They know what their roles and accountabilities should be. That's what they do-and that's all they do. They knew, even before Peter Ducker suggested it, that managing is full-time work, not just something you do when you have finished your real work. It is difficult for some managers to realize that even with all the policies, procedures, rules, operating manuals, and systems multi-level organizations will not run themselves.

To say that multi-level organizations need to be managed seems patently obvious. It's like saying that your car won't run unless you do some things to keep it going. However, talking to an automotive mechanic about the approach some people use to servicing and maintaining their car can be an enlightening experience. Such things as "How about putting four quarts of oil in now so I won't have to stop so often for more," or "Since we may run into snow in a hundred miles or so, could you put the chains on now?" or "While you're rotating the tires could you also change the air? It's the original air and probably pretty bad by now."

Supervisors can tell you similar stories about managers who do the same things to their organizations.

> "Because one person continually has trouble with the phone system, my boss required all people in the department attend a two-day telephone training program."

"We constantly get 'raised fist' policies from our manager. When something doesn't go right, she raises her fist and shouts, 'From now on, there will be no more....' and a new policy is born."

"We now have a new sign-in, sign-out policy for anytime we leave the office area, even for lunch, the restroom, or coffee. The boss read in a management book that some horrendous amount of productivity is lost because of 'unscheduled absences'."

While it is more common to undermanage through the issuance of policies, procedures, and rules, truly successful managers work hard to follow a basic truth: it is as possible to overmanage into disaster as it is to undermanage into disaster.

One common way to do this came to our attention during a management seminar we were conducting. In one of our discussions, a class member, Tom Haskins, suddenly slapped his forehead and dragged his hand slowly down his face. To seminar leaders, that's not a particularly positive gesture. What did we say that could have been so unsettling to Tom? On the next break, he explained his reaction. He indicated that we had given him the solution to a problem that had been bothering him for some time. "Two years ago," he explained, "I headed the Actuarial Department in our company. When the Board of Directors named me president, I immediately selected Bill Phillips to be my successor in the Actuarial Department because he had done a great job for several years as the assistant department manager.

"Not wanting to let my promotion change my relationships too drastically, I continued my habit of spending a half-hour a day in the cafeteria shooting the breeze with the people I'd worked with before my promotion. Naturally, we talked about whatever pot was boiling in their department at the time. The actuarial problems were very familiar to me and frankly talking about them was more fun and relaxing than having to deal with what was waiting for me in my office. What I came to realize was that Bill was using these discussions to make decisions in his department.

"Because I thought Bill Phillips was very capable," Tom continued somewhat sheepishly, "it came as quite a shock to discover that the man was not making decisions on his own and perhaps was not able to do. I realized that in absentia I was running the Actuarial Department as well as the president's office. When I came to this seminar, I'd about decided to replace Bill because I felt he was not doing his job.

"The light came on when you were talking about over-managing. That's exactly what I was doing. I'm the reason why Bill is not making decisions. I have been managing his department from the cafeteria, saying things as president in front of his people that 'dictated' his decision or undermined decisions he had already made. It's funny. I could never see it before but now it's plain as day. And am I relieved. All it will take to bring out Bill's real capabilities and restore his confidence and authority is for me to sleep in for an extra half-hour each morning".

In talking to Tom a few months later, he said Bill Phillips was doing an outstanding job running the Actuarial Department now that Tom has stopped his early morning sessions around the coffee pot. "I still go to the cafeteria sessions now and then," he said, "because I want to maintain a degree of visibility, but you can bet that we don't talk about actuarial problems anymore."

One of the traits of outstanding managers is that they recognize easy solutions when they see them. Many management problems can be solved as effortlessly as Tom's by following a few very simple but important precepts:never scorn a solution because it seems so easy.

Great managers have acquired a discipline that limits managers to managing and resists the common and sometimes overpowering temptation to do everybody else's job at the same time. They have developed that sense of balance that allows them to manage full-time while getting others to learn and do what they get paid to do. The manager who does too much or too little managing is often easy to spot. They either use an elephant gun to kill a mouse or they don't know the mice exist until they have overrun the premises.

Great managers know that their success is determined not so much by who they are but by what they do.

In working with middle managers over the years, we have found that few of the traditional indicators of success have any significant correlation to managerial success. Intelligence? By itself intelligence is a weak indicator. We have seen highly intelligent people who have failed miserably as managers. We have also seen those with average intelligence go a long way in the managerial ranks. One's IQ is a score on an intelligence test; it does not measure logic, business acumen, or street smarts.

Education? There are as many Harvard MBAs who have not made it up the management ladder as there are nondegreed dropouts who have. A senior vice president in a large commercial bank became famous-or infamous-in Los Angeles banking circles with his oft-repeated comment, "I got where I am today without ever setting foot in a classroom."

Leadership style? The respective successes and failures of democratic leaders, consensus- builders, and benevolent dictators make it evident that no single style of leadership is an effective predictor of managerial success.

There has been a great deal of research and writing relative to identifying characteristics of successful managers and leaders. From these efforts a number of profiles and indexes have been generated. The problem, of course, is that the profiles and indexes are inconsistent themselves and individuals rarely possess all the characteristics of any of them. It's that common situation in which the average does not really fit anyone. It's like the five hunters who shoot at a duck and gleefully exclaim, as the duck flies away, "On the average, that bird is dead."

We are certainly not suggesting that these characteristics-education, intelligence, and leadership style-are not important in managing or in any other job. We are suggesting that with or without these characteristics successful managers become great on the basis of actions and performance, regardless of their profile or credentials. Great managers know their strengths and exploit them; they also know their weaknesses and work hard to overcome or compensate for them. They fill their personal voids by hiring or training others to perform in those areas, by managing that performance, and by further developing their own strengths.

Great managers know that their people and the integrity of their organizational structure are their greatest assets.

They recognize that a significant part of their job is not only to maximize the performance of their people but also to develop them, to prepare them for greater responsibilities and future changes, to reduce their limitations and stretch their capabilities. There's nothing particularly new about these managerial responsibilities. Every management textbook says the same thing. What they don't say, however, is that the best way to develop people is to coach, support, and counsel them to improve and grow in their current positions. People develop on the job-not in the classroom, not by role-playing versions of a fictional future, not by assessment-center profiles, nor by rotational look-see assignments-but by becoming the very best they can at what they are currently being paid to do.

Good people are the most valuable resource for any manager. But the key value of any resource is not its existence but how it's used. The unemployment line is filled with those managers who live by the axiom that "you are only as good as your people." Great managers know that developing good people is only the beginning. The real measure of managerial ability is the utilization of those people. What are they being developed to become? When we ask that question of successful managers, the most common response is "self-reliant" and "independent"-not as personal characteristics but as performance traits. The managers did not mean independence and self-reliance in the sense that they should solve problems and make decisions without anybody else's help but in the sense that they have the confidence and ability to seek out and exploit the expertise necessary to make sound decisions and solve performance problems. "I want to develop my people so that they don't come to my office before they solve the problem or make the decision unless I'm the expert or the counselor they need," said one manager. "I want to see them after the fact so I can keep up on things and so that we can learn what can be learned from the situation." As another manager put it, "I want to develop managers who can make managerial decisions, supervisors who can make supervisory decisions, and workers who can make work decisions. And be right - most of the time."

In addition, great managers know that all of this talk about development and proper utilization of people is so much nonsense without the organizational resources and a strong organizational structure to support it. Business folklore to the contrary, great managers know that consistently improving performance and developing people can only occur in an organizational structure that both defines and limits the authority that can be exercised within that structure. Common practices that subordinate the structure-end-runs, midnight requisitions, order and command-are quick fix Band-Aids that in the long run tend to redefine and weaken the structure.

Outstanding managers work very hard to produce an organizational environment in which lines of authority and communications are clear and in which all management personnel have access to the resources needed for self-reliance and independence. They recognize that staff and service groups are invaluable resources but serve in an advisory capacity only. They recognize that plans should be developed, decisions made, and problems solved within the organizational structure, including those decisions to refer some decisions and problems elsewhere.

Finally, they recognize that organizational structures are fluid and dynamic rather than static graphics on an organization chart. Organizational interactions, political infighting, and performance pressures often bend and sometimes break existing structures, reducing their effectiveness. For these reasons, outstanding managers devote considerable time and attention to monitoring the decision-making and communication processes within the existing organizational structure. Often this requires doing battle with those who would usurp authority and those who would abdicate it. It may require demanding service and staff support when it's not forthcoming or is poorly conducted. On occasion, refining the organizational structure may mean modifying and redefining it to fit changing needs and organizational circumstances.

Great managers know that an effective management structure is one in which each level has both common and unique accountabilities.

Certain areas of accountability cut across all management levels. They are simply applied to a broader base of people and greater scope of responsibility as one moves up the organizational ladder. Common accountabilities are well established in most organizations. Unique accountabilities at each level, however, are rarely established.

For example, most organizations do very well in identifying the "how tos" that all managers and supervisors are supposed to be adept at carrying out. Witness the tremendous amount of time and money spent on training the "ings" of management: planning, organizing, delegating, communicating, motivating, and so forth. Similarly, significant attention is given to the technology of the function that is being managed and supervised. The "how tos" and the functional technology are the common areas of management responsibilities that do not differ from one level of management to another. Highly successful managers know, however, that equal time and attention should also be allocated to identifying the unique accountabilities-in other words, the "whats" of managing and supervising. Unless managers and supervisors know the "whats" of their jobs, the "how tos" are impossible to apply effectively.

See if the following scene isn't familiar. It's Friday morning and Diane is called into her boss' office and told that she has been promoted to supervisor. After the kind words and congratulatory comments have been exchanged, Diane asks when she is to start on her new job. "Why, Monday morning, of course," replies the boss, as though something magical is going to happen over the weekend to convert her from mission worker to supervisor.

Diane arrives Monday morning, properly dressed for her new management role, shoulders back, a smile on her face, and walks into her new office. She spends the morning getting the office in shape-files organized, desk arranged, pictures on the wall. She returns from lunch, stands in the middle of her office and says to herself, "Now what do I do?" She takes the question to her new boss, who replies, "Well you know that there are certain reports to fill out, you need to check the work going on, help your people when they have problems. Things like that. Once you're settled in, we'll schedule you for the company's supervisory training program. That will give you what you need to know."

With the help of the mission workers, the secretary, and the memory of what her supervisor used to spend time doing, Diane develops her supervisory routine. A couple of months later she is notified of her registration in the supervisory training program. She attends and learns a great deal about planning, decision-making, delegating, and so forth. She reports to her boss, "That was great training. I can now plan, make decisions, and delegate with the best of them. However, boss, I have a problem."

"Oh," says the boss. "What's your problem?"

"I don't know what I should plan, what decisions I can make, and what I can delegate," replies Diane.

This scenario is repeated just as often at the managerial level as it is at the supervisory level. Knowing the "hows" of a management job is of little value if the supervisor or manager does not know to what those skills should be applied. Artisans will tell you that they are not judged by the skills they possess but by the products those skills produce. The outstanding manager will tell you the same about managing and supervising-the end product is the measure of one's skill and the means by which performance is judged. To tell supervisors and managers, or to imply by omission of any other directions, that your job is to plan, make decisions, and delegate is like telling a carpenter that you want him or her to hammer, plane, and saw. Great managers know that one of the first things anybody needs on the job is a clear understanding of what they are accountable for and what their unique contributions to the organization are expected to be. Most organizations do a good job of this at the mission worker level; they give little or no attention to it at management levels.

We often conduct seminars in which both managers and supervisors are present. We ask participants in each management level to define that level, i.e. supervisors to define supervision, managers define managing. We even go so far as to ask them to write a definition of their level that differentiates it from other levels, identifying what is unique about the accountabilities at their level. Invariability their definitions are strikingly similar, with little or no differentiation between the levels. It is as though managing is the same as supervising.

Moreover, the definitions do not exclude mission workers and top management. For example, a common definition is getting things done through others or words to that effect. Our response to that definition is, "Should supervisors get things done through others? Should mission workers get things done through others? How about top management?" Of course they should. As a matter of fact, getting things done through others is a universal practice, a fact of every day life outside the workplace. Anyone who is married and/or has children can attest to that.

Some of the most common management and supervisory problems that organizations have can be attributed in large measure to the practice of painting all levels with the same brush. Duplication of efforts and resources, diffusion of accountabilities, misallocation of resources, muddled lines of authority and communication, supervisors doing the work of those they supervise, and managers supervising rather than managing-all are common outcomes of each management level being defined as little more than a grown-up version of the level below.

Highly successful managers know how to get things done and, more importantly, how to get their people to get things done.

The management philosophy that says, "The better I manage, the less work I'll have to do" has a ring of half-truth to it. It would be better stated, "The better I manage, the less of my subordinates' work I'll have to do."

While common management skills are important in getting subordinates to respond to performance and organizational demands, most of those skills are carried out in what we call the formal environment; that is, they involve processes and procedures, schedules, meetings, memos, and reports. They have a commonality about them, a predictability as to process if not to substance. Project plans are strikingly similar in form regardless of the nature of the project and the people doing them. Templates exist for processes and procedures, recurring reports, and meeting schedules and agendas. Activities in the formal environment tend to occur according to schedules and plans as if whatever work is involved can wait until the scheduled time. They are in a sense a part of the wallpaper and the pattern doesn't change much from wall to wall and company to company. Because these activities are formal and predictable, they don't really have the impact most managers think they have in communicating and maintaining priorities.

In order to provide clear direction and to maintain priorities, great managers have learned to supplement formal activities with informal ones. The informal environment includes those arenas in which communication occurs spontaneously, unscheduled and seemingly unplanned. The hallways, the parking lot, the cafeteria, the subordinate's office, the production floor-places where the manager arrives unannounced and a work conversation ensues.

Effective managers know that work conversations in the informal environment have a significantly greater impact on the subordinate than communications that occur in staff meetings or by memo. They have experienced or heard about situations such as that which occurred at a large manufacturing company. The president was leaving on a four-week vacation in Europe. As he was walking to his car, he noticed that there were papers and leaves strewn about the parking lot. In a side comment to one of his senior VPs, he said, "What a mess this parking lot is." When he returned four weeks later, the parking lot had been repaved, with new curbing and landscaping.

Or the situation at a large construction company where a senior VP was touring a new construction site. Along the side of the road leading to the site were several portable toilets, most of which were mud-splattered and dented and with doors secured by bailing wire. The senior VP, again in a side comment, said to one of his subordinates, "I wonder how many of those we have in the system?" Three weeks later he received a forty-page report complete with charts and graphs, detailing the number, size, condition, age and replacement costs of all the portable toilets in the system." Compare that scene with one in which, during a staff meeting, the senior VP says to the subordinate manager, "John, I want a report, complete with charts and graphs, of the number, condition, etcetera, of all the portable toilets in the system. John will certainly accept the assignment, but there are two things he'll be certain of: the project will not be very high on his or the senior VP's priority list, and the old man's elevator does not go all the way to the top.

Managers who have been around the block a few times have been embarrassed by these kinds of situations more than once and have learned to be cautious about comments made in informal situations. The outstanding managers, as they tend to do, have learned by these experiences that the informal environment is itself a management tool. They have learned to plan to be spontaneous as a technique for reinforcing priorities. Blending the power of the informal environment with the planning, organizing, and communicating skills used in the formal environment is one of the high-order management skills that truly successful managers have developed.

Another example of the effective use of the informal, or spontaneous, environment occurred during one of our middle management seminars. We were discussing the concept of routine and pay-off duties and how to maintain a reasonable balance between the two. One of the participants offered a technique to allow payoff duties to compete successfully with routine ones. His way of expressing the technique was, "Let It Win Occasionally." The "it" in this case is the payoff duty. Let the payoff duty win occasionally over the routine activity. In further explanation, he posed the following scenario to the class: "Let's say you're meeting with one or more of your supervisors to begin planning a specific payoff activity. During the meeting, your boss calls and says, 'we've got a major problem. I need you in my office immediately.' How many of you could say the following to your boss and not get fired? 'Boss, I'm having a very important meeting with my supervisors. Can you give me about ten minutes?' Even if the boss says no, you've still sent a pretty strong message to your supervisors about the importance of the payoff activity."

Great managers know that they have a gold mine in their own backyard.

Running a multi-level organization is a costly business. As departments grow, so do the demands for additional resources. The reflex response of many managers is to hike up the budget requests beyond what is reasonable and play the other traditional organizational games when they know their proposed budgets will be cut or not approved at all.

The great managers do something quite different. They submit reasonable budget requests and then fight hard for their approval. In addition, they know that as their organization grows and as time, conditions, and economic circumstances change, certain inefficiencies will have crept into their organization. Not in the sense of mindless waste from people not doing good work, but of systems that no longer meet the needs of the organization, reports that have become superfluous, and objectives that are no longer attainable. Any of these situations represent mis-allocated resources. These resources, once released from noncontributing activities, can be applied to those that support the growth of the organization or spur it to even greater performance.

Outstanding managers were practicing "Intrapreneurship" long before it became a popular buzzword in management literature and boardrooms. Great managers have learned to seek gold in their own backyards rather than, or certainly before, embarking on the arduous task of trying to mine it from the company's or the industry's lode.

These then are concepts and practices that separate the great managers from the merely adequate ones. How will you know the great managers when you see them? You certainly won't identify them walking down the hall or by checking their credentials or by their longevity in management. The best indicator that we know of is the one mentioned at the beginning of this chapter. You identify great managers by the results they produce over an extended period of time. Great managers have a record of consistently good results, both from their own efforts and those of their departments, regardless of the problems, pressures and unusual demands to which they and their departments may have been subjected.

Other less successful managers will tend to show a pattern of results with peaks and valleys corresponding to good and bad times, economic upswings, and cost cuts. How often we've seen an unexpected project or unpredictable problem such as a new safety mandate, equipment changeover, personnel reduction, or mechanical breakdown cause a department to literally go to pieces. Departments run by outstanding managers will absorb these demands without skipping a beat and without missing a deadline. The best way to identify the great managers is find those whose performance and that of their organizations seem unaffected by the pressures and demands that surround them. The traits and talents they have are not visible at a glance. They cannot be bottled or bought or put into systems that are then drip-fed into the less talented.

Fortunately, these traits and talents tend to be behavioral in nature and can be learned. The first step, however, is to identify these traits and talents and to describe them in as much detail as possible. That is what we have attempted to do in this chapter. Learning and practicing the basics of organization management and opportunity management are the first steps in the process of becoming a great manager.

CHAPTER SEVEN

THE POWER BROKERS

For the past four decades a trend has emerged in American business that has quietly but persistently weakened the once-strong ties that bound the organizational structure. Once a nation proud of its manufacturing prowess, and of the people who built our products, we have evolved to a condition in which manufacturing and operations hold the lowest position on the organizational power train. No self-respecting Harvard or Stanford MBA or management "fast-tracker" would spend more than a quick, cursory rotation on the front lines. The key positions of influence are at the top of the organizational structure, sitting at the right hand of the greed mongers, the bean counters, and the other believers in magic. The best places to learn the trappings of power are in high-level-staff power positions.

One of the fundamental lessons in Business 101 is that staff positions are advisory only, their strength residing in providing expertise to line managers for the sole purpose of assisting those managers to meet their operating goals. Staff positions were conceived to be behind-the-scenes experts in specialties where operating managers could not be expected to be experts. Specialized resources could then be brought to bear on the fundamental purpose of the business: to sell the company's products or provide their services.

So much for theory. Our experience shows power does not come through advisory positions. But look at the potential for power that comes from holding a position that talks directly to top management and that has access into every department in the organization. The temptations to slide into positions of authority are simply too great. The tendency is for staff groups to take on more and more direct decision-making power. To the detriment of the organization, top management allows and even encourages them to do so. The net result has been that authority and accountability that once rightfully resided with line departments now belongs to staff groups. Safety Departments have assumed accountability for safe performance in the workplace; Quality Assurance Departments for the quality of products and services; Human Resources Departments for everything human. The most distressing example is the extent to which Information Systems and technology groups have assumed such a formidable position of power in almost every department in most organizations. Anyone who has been told that his or her computer upgrade won't be finished for another week while unanswered customer inquiries continue to pile up can attest to the stranglehold that computer departments can exert.

This assumption of power and authority did not take place through top management mandate, but rather through a process of power grabbing by staff groups, and abdication of accountability by management. Admittedly, to a degree, this trend is the result of increased government intrusion into business and a myriad of new legislation, as well as the administrative time and paperwork that have resulted. Legal blackmail under the guise of political correctness has forced organizations to rely heavily on staff groups such as Human Resources and Legal to deal with issues that are considered beyond the expertise and ability of line departments.

A case study presented in the March-April 1998 issue of Harvard Business Review illustrates the divergent opinions by organizational gurus on the role of staff functions. In this typical Harvard Business case study, the central issue around which the case evolved was, "What should the Human Resources Department do?" The central figure in the case was Robinson, a human relations manager who had come to the organization from the field of consulting. Two responses to the case represented opposite views. Professor Edward E. Lawler III wrote, "The first thing I would do is remind him that he used to be an excellent consultant.

Then I would try to make him understand that to succeed in his current position, he needs to return to that role." Of course this is the right answer - theoretically, practically, and by any sense of logic.

A diametrically opposed view was expressed by Tim Riley who wrote, "First, he has to approach his job differently. Robinson has a consultant's mind-set he needs to lose, and begin to think and behave like a manager." There is no way to know what Mr. Riley means by "think and behave like a manager." But if we take the generally accepted approach, Mr. Riley wants Robinson not to be an advisor to management, an internal consultant to line organization, but rather a promoter of ideas, a fighter for "the cause," an advocate of the latest theories, and a social experimenter. It is no wonder that staff functions act with total power and little responsibility; there are too many Tim Rileys and not enough Edward Lawler, IIIs in today's business world.

The Empire Builders

Power begets empires-and staff groups have built dynasties over the years. What better way to staff an operation, provide administrative support and office facilities (for the large number of people necessary to monitor safety or quality or purchasing) than from a centralized staff location? And what more convenient way to make decisions accordingly?

A case study based on two West Coast financial institutions illustrates how empires can be built and how they can very easily be destroyed. We call the case, "Ups and Downs."

Five years ago, Marv O'Luss became the training director of Consolidated Diversified. During the first three years, he established himself at the head of what he called a "dynamic, active training organization." During that time, he received the support and backing of his boss, Sharon Glory, and was able to accomplish the following:

- Eighteen staff members with graduate degrees in instructional technology and industrial psychology were hired. His staff had a great many ideas about what the organization needed. These ideas were translated into a variety of training programs.

- To assure that his staff of professionals were not distracted from their main duty of designing and conducting training programs, Marv personally handled all training discussions with line management. To assure that he was always in the best position to coordinate his various programs with the needs of line management, he required that all contacts go through him. In this way, he reasoned, line management could look to one person on training matters without the confusion of a variety of professional advisors.

- Marv had achieved control of the corporate training budget so that all training had to go through him for approval. He wanted to be sure that no inadequate training would go on and the available money was spent on the courses he and his staff provided.

- One line department head quit the company in the second year of Marv's directorship when she could not get approval for a series of training programs she wanted for her department. Both Sharon Glory, Marv's boss, and the president backed Marv very strongly. The department head commented that she couldn't run her department if she didn't have control of the training her people needed and should receive. The president countered that Marv was the training expert and his advice should be heeded. This evidence of Marv's support from the president was all it took for other department heads to fall in line.

- In the middle of the third year Marv finally got approval from top management to build a sophisticated corporate university. The building was a show place of training technology. There was a large video studio; every classroom was equipped with the latest computers and distance-learning technology and a monitoring system in Marv's office; rear-screen projection, electric boards, console-controlled lighting, electric student response systems were everywhere to be seen. There were two large auditoriums and a suite of offices for Marv, his trainers, the secretaries, courses coordinators, sound/video technicians, and service personnel.

- Marv submitted a plan to Sharon for adding a number of trainers and support personnel to each of the plants and field offices across the country, all of who reported back to Marv at the corporate office.

Marv was proud of the evidence of management support of his training vision. He was pleased that the training department was right on schedule with the objectives he had for it: a large and diversified staff of great instructors teaching exciting" frontier" courses, a model physical plant, and strong support from the top.

It may appear from the outside looking in that Marv was indeed doing a marvelous job in managing his department. However, a careful analysis of his situation with specific attention to the role of line and staff groups in an organization reveals some major problems that Marv would undoubtedly face when tough times occurred.

In an addendum to the case study, we describe what did happen when tough times occurred.

"A monetary squeeze has hit the company. The President has announced that the company will take a $40 million loss for the quarter and will have to downsize by about 5000 employees.

The Operating Committee, charged with righting the ship, has cut everyone's budget, especially Marv's. It seems that no one present attempted to protect Marv's training budget. Some of the senior managers made statements like:

> 'Now is a good time to cut back on that training empire. It is great for showing visitors, but we never got much good from that department.'

> 'My people told me that they send the people they could best afford to excuse to these courses because, if they didn't, they were branded as obstructionists and not committed to the development of their people.'

> 'There's no need for a university within the corporation. There are five real ones within driving distance of headquarters.'

When the president asked his senior managers to cite value received from the training given to their people, only a few examples were given along with positive remarks about a series of skill courses that had been going on before Marv joined the company.

Most of Marv's training staff had already given their notices. Although there are still some courses to teach, they feel that they should seek employment in companies where training expertise can be utilized both inside and outside the classroom.

Evidence has been building that some very real operating problems could have been overcome with training. When asked by the president why it had not been done, the senior managers replied, 'Training is Marv's area. He never really asked us what we wanted or needed. When we asked, Marv's answer tended to be that it wasn't in the current budget.' This situation caused strong counter-factions working to erode Marv's stature with the president.

The 'university' classrooms now stand largely empty. The training staff is down to Marv, a secretary, and one sales instructor. Skill training has been transferred to the respective line departments. The equipment is being sold and the company wants to find a buyer for the 'university.' Marv, too, is on the market...are you interested?"

Good facilities and bright people in staff functions are not at issue in this case nor in our view of staff departments. How these facilities and people are used to support the operating organizations is the key concept. Marv is the epitome of the staff managers who seek to create power by pandering to top management for "support", accumulating resources and staffing far beyond what's necessary and providing services that satisfy the staff specialty but do little for the line organization. What does it matter that we already have line managers and supervisors on site who should be accountable for all of those areas? What do they know about these highly specialized functions? The prevailing attitude is that they only supervise the work and can use all of the help they can get.

There is no argument that line management needs all the help they can get from staff specialties. But the key word is "help": advice, suggestions, recommendations, expertise, service-all of those things that staff groups are paid to provide. When advice turns into power, authority, and no accountability, the effects on the organization can be devastating.

Dave Ulrick expressed another disturbing point of view in his article, "A New Mandate for Human Resources," appearing in the January-February issues, 1995 of the Harvard Business Review. Ulrich wrote that, "There is good reason for HR's beleaguered reputation. It is often ineffective, incompetent, and costly; in a phrase, it is value sapping." While there may be merit to his statement, his solutions are questionable since these so called solutions were a primary cause of HR departments becoming "ineffective, incompetent, and costly." Mr. Ulrich suggests, "Achieving organizational excellence must be the work of HR." Why? Where did HR get the accountability for "organizational excellence?" Organizational excellence means providing and delivering a good product and servicing the customer properly. HR doesn't even see a customer. Yet Ulrich suggests that HR must be the source for adding value to the organization in dealing with customers, investors, and employees-all the issues for which line management is accountable and should be doing on a daily basis.

It is interesting that in the same issue of the Harvard Business Review another case study, entitled "The Empowerment Effort that Came Undone," appeared. Mary V. Gelinas and Roger G. James wrote, "Improvement initiatives fail when consultants lead them." How true it is. The fact is that any initiative, improvement or otherwise, led by consultants, external or internal, from any staff departments, will fail-guaranteed.

For most employees it is laughable that the staff departments maintain that they exist to "serve" the line organization, yet line organizations too often are ordered or choose to follow orders from staff groups. That is a unique definition of "serving!"

THE FADS OF THE DAY

Staff advice and services, however well meaning, often create chaos and misdirection. Staff personnel too often act on the fads of the day, rather than on the needs of the business. Questionable advice from misguided staff has forced many organizations to struggle through a series of questionable "special management programs" in the past three decades. A recent example of staff advice is Ford Motor Company's plan to pay low-performing workers to quit. This plan has all the characteristics of staff advice (USA Today, July 16, 1998.) Batia Wiesenfeld, an assistant professor of management at New York University is quoted: "Look at what this does to morale. You're rewarding people for being bad performers." These programs along with many others of the past have failed to help improve basic business functions. They have cost the companies involved a great deal of time, and money, and have caused confusion and employee alienation.

"Employees are cynical & angry about the constant parade of initiatives that come with the usual aura of imminent importance," reported by Rich Moran & George Bailey of Sibson & Co. (Daily News, January 18, 1993.) "Line and field employees," they reported, "view staff positions as simply siphoning off money that could be better used to buy a new truck or to up-date a plant. Employees want to know how staff serves them, and what staff's role is in serving the customer."

Staff positions have never been able to communicate the need for their existence properly. Members of staff functions often feel that the reason they cannot explain their function is that the line management is not smart enough, or concerned enough to understand it. Therefore, staff feels that they understand the situation well and they know the right prescriptions. They constantly come up with programs that they impose upon the organization, most often with the blessing of the top management.

The Sensitivity Training of the 1960s, based on Carl Roger's theories, is a classic example of staff making a recommendation that had devastating effects. This program disabled and debased many managers. Peter Drucker was one among many who was very critical of Sensitivity Training. He said that, "I'm one of those very simple people who believe that one is not entitled to inflict damage on the living body. For the weak, the lame, the defenseless, the shy, the vulnerable, this is a very dangerous thing. The real sadists, the wolves, tear the little lambs to pieces. The casualty rate is unacceptable." (*Drucker, The Man Who Invented the Corporate Society* by John J. Tarrut). It is our hope that the Sensitivity Training currently in vogue for every public official who is guilty of political incorrectness is different than the Rogers' version.

Later in the 1970s, the search for something new by the staff people produced the infamous Quality Circles, a concept copied after the Japanese style of management of the time. That fiasco, which still has a few die-hard followers, did not cause the type of people problems that Sensitivity Training did. However, the whole approach proved to be little more than a waste of valuable time and money, further diminishing the confidence of employees toward management's dedication to solving work problems.

Total Quality Management (TQM), Teamwork, and Empowerment are fads of more current vintage. Many companies have made a very expensive, long-term commitment to making these approaches work. Some have achieved acceptable results, occasionally offering dramatic improvements. But for most organizations, it has meant a series of training programs, establishing committee after committee, and working tirelessly on meaningless projects. Often these unrealized promises gave employees the impression that they were really going to run the organization, even in the areas where they had little knowledge, skill, or understanding. The promise was that all employees were going to have a say in the nature and the scope of the business, a promise so broad and vague that it could not and should not be fulfilled.

The reason, and potential value, for having staff people is to listen to their advice because they are experts in their fields. However, if the advice is purely theoretical, lacking relevance and practicality in the operating units, or is not accompanied by realistic implementation processes, the advice is at best useless and at worst dangerous.

Staff groups are cost centers and yet occupy a

unique position on the organizational chart. They have a direct line to the top and thus compete with the operating organization for resources of all types, including access to top management. In this position, staff groups can wield significantly more influence and power than their area of specialty commands. The result is a tendency for resource allocations to be severely unbalanced, with operating departments left to struggle with less funds, machinery, and manpower. It often takes a major recession or a loss of profit to rectify this situation. It's no wonder that staff groups are the first to go when the crunch hits-not because they are unimportant but because they have been allowed to grow out of proportion to their value.

The best of all worlds, of course, is to prevent the abnormal growth and influence of staff groups from occurring in the first place. This is top management's responsibility. They should determine the policy on the role of staff groups, their accountability and their relationship to other departments. In a perfect world, the operating departments would make all operating and personnel decisions. Even though this is not a perfect world, the principle should be followed with exceptions noted when circumstances demand a decision by staff. Line managers should consult with the staff people when relevant decisions have to be made and agree on the best approach to implementation. To avoid future organizational chaos, staff advice should not be blindly implemented, no matter how good it sounds. Blind trust in staff leads to a confusing, and thus detrimental, reversal of accountability and authority.

The IBM Story

IBM, before Mr. Gerstner took over, is a classic example of allowing staff functions to dominate the workings of an organization. Associated Press published an interview on February 8, 1993, in which John Cunnif talked with Eugene Jennings, Professor Emeritus of Business Management at Michigan State. Mr. Jennings, according to the Associated Press, was a consultant to IBM for thirty years, a remarkable record of longevity for any consultant. Mr. Jennings believed that there was no "all-purpose" explanation for IBM's problems, but one came close: "IBM failed to manage the fundamentals." This statement is extremely important because IBM's dilemma was not caused by a failure in technology.

IBM's management philosophy was merely a reflection of its marketing approach, pushed forcefully through the organization and via speeches outside the organization by large numbers of aggressive marketing people. This marketing approach was based on a set of questionable criteria:

1. The IBM way is the only way.

2. The staff knows best what is good for the line.

3. IBM's marketing approach is a model for other departments and other organizations to follow.

4. No improvements are to be made on IBM's plan unless it is decided so by the gurus in the staff functions.

5. Every function in IBM is subordinate to marketing.

6. Those who don't believe in the IBM way are not going to be around long.

7. Those who agree to the IBM way will be paid very generously.

"The measure of success," Mr. Jennings maintained, "was how fast one could move both laterally and vertically. This being so, managers learned more about the art of mobility than management."

Actually IBM became a company that was more interested in keeping people from making mistakes than allowing them to take actions in the areas that the IBM staff plan didn't cover. The end result was staff control of every aspect of sales, personal life, thought, dress, and physical appearance. Their motto was "Think." They never indicated to the public what and how. For IBM employees, ironically, both the "what" and "how" were under control of Big Blue.

As it did at IBM, the lesson comes home again and again that fundamentals of management are not to be tinkered with:

1. Value the customer, internal and external.

2. Increase employee focus on customer satisfaction not technological monopoly.

3. Operate the entire organization by line management with individual accountability for performance.

4. Create a lean organization, responsive to the economics of the business, the industry, and to human values.

5. Have lean staff functions, with highly qualified personnel charged with assisting line management not dictating to them

6. Establish crystal-clear objectives at each level of the organization and in each operating unit.

A similar but more specific line versus staff problem existed in a warehousing company in the San Francisco

Bay area. For years, the company had a significant problem with lost-time accidents and downtime caused by safety violations. The safety director at the time was held accountable by the warehouse manager for all aspects of safety and took his job very seriously. He spent countless hours driving around the facility in a golf cart, observing and correcting unsafe conditions and practices. To increase his visibility, he wore a green hardhat with a white cross.

The attitude of the warehousemen toward the safety director was best exemplified by one who remarked, "The safest place at any point in time was wherever the green hat was. Anywhere else, you take your life in your hands." But the green hat could only be at one place at one time.

The safety director retired and a replacement was hired. During his first meeting with the warehouse manager, the manager said, "Welcome aboard. I want you to know that you have my support for your safety programs."

"That's interesting," replied the safety director, "I was going to say the same thing to you. You have my support for your safety programs."

They went back and forth with who was going to support whom until finally the manager got the message. He was accountable for safety and it was indeed his safety program.

The manager communicated that message to his management team. The following year the warehouse won a national safety award for the greatest decrease in lost-time accidents. And duplicated that record for the next three years. Why? Because now everyone was accountable for safety and could be in all places at all times.

While we know of no companies that have gone under because of undue authority vested in staff groups, we do know that there is a price to pay when the condition exists. The price is decreased influence by line managers and supervisors, authority without responsibility, organizational elephantiasis, and abdication of responsibility.

Decreased Influence of Managers and Supervisors

Production has been shown to suffer when line managers and supervisors have to check with a staff group before making a decision that effects their day-by-day operations. It suffers when their response to employees about everyday operating questions or problems is "Let me call staff about that." It suffers when work is delayed because staff decisions or lack of prompt service stymies managers and supervisors. When these circumstances are multiplied by the number of staff groups in the organization, the net effect has to be a perception of line managers and supervisors as "flunkies" and "message carriers." That perception is bad enough. The real price, however, is the effect on production. It has been well documented that employee perception of their supervisor's influence in the organization is reflected in their performance. An image of low influence tends to result in lower productivity; an image of high influence tends to result in increased production. When the employees feel that "when the boss talks, management listens," all aspects of their jobs and their productivity are positively affected.

Authority without Responsibility

The narrow specialties of staff groups and the authority they are given produce an anomaly that has serious consequences for the true mission of the organization. When staff groups have the authority to make any decisions involving the work of other departments, they have the ultimate weapon in the power arsenal. Power to stop production and to impose decisions without suffering the consequences of their actions. Finance managers who arbitrarily impose cost and overtime restrictions are not held liable for production shortfalls or missed shipping dates. Rather, they are often rewarded for having met cost containment goals. On the other hand, operating managers who did not meet their goals because of financial restrictions are often criticized if not reprimanded. Similar situations occur when QA or Safety managers unilaterally stop production, impose arbitrary restrictions, or modify procedures to satisfy their own agenda.

Organizational Elephantiasis

Elephantiasis is a tropical disease that causes a grotesque swelling of the extremities. The "disease" begins to creep into organizations when staff groups feel the need to decentralize and provide positions for their members within the actual operating departments. The work of holding meetings, gathering data, writing reports, monitoring operations, and other "busywork" that staff departments are famous for creating, all require on-site personnel. When this happens, more people are hired and show up on the organizational chart in just about every major department and facility. This, however, is not quite elephantiasis; it's simply organizational obesity. It becomes elephantiasis when the staff's on-site staff members find that they are not well received in the field, that they cannot communicate well because they speak a language only other staff members can understand, and that their directives meet stony resistance or reluctant compliance. Thus, paralysis through elephantiasis results.

In addition, organizational elephantiasis becomes more firmly entrenched when on-site staff members find that their only safe haven is in the presence of other staff members. They then begin to communicate among themselves, sending reports to each other and to the home office, and essentially distancing themselves from the operating organization to which they were assigned. The result tends to be the development of an eerie ghost organization-one that parallels the real organization but functions outside of it. Besides the outrageously high cost and waste of human resources, the potentially fatal symptom of the disease is that the real organization can dry up and blow away while the ghost organization can ostensibly go on and on forever, particularly in large bureaucratic organizations. When their allegiance is only to themselves and to their narrow specialty (i.e. computer departments for computer specialists or finance departments for financial experts), the costs in terms of human resources and the loss of specialized expertise to the operating organization is staggering.

Abdication of Responsibility

More often than not the operating departments to which the staff directives apply resist those directives, either overtly or covertly. Very often the resistance is warranted. Middle management should take their case to top management for review and, when merited, overturn the staff directive. However, when top management sides consistently and arbitrarily with staff groups, as they often do, the operating managers soon learn not to beat their heads against the wall. They simply go with the flow. This is a classic case of abdication in the face of a no-win situation. The door is now open for staff groups to march in and freely wreak the havoc they are so capable of producing.

Abdication also occurs when staff groups offer to carry out unpleasant or specialized tasks for which line managers or supervisors are accountable. "How about if I work out that budget for you just to show you how it's done?" or "Since you're a new supervisor and I'm experienced in HR matters, how about if I carry out that disciplinary discussion with your mission worker?" There aren't many line managers or supervisors who would turn down such offers. From these kinds of scenarios evolves a pattern of staff groups routinely continuing to carry out these activities, however pure their motives may be.

Hayes, Wheelwright, and Clark, in their book, *Dynamic Manufacturing*, identify the misguided role of staff functions very well. They succinctly state, "A large staff, composed of ambitious and overprotective people determined to justify their existence, make work and make trouble. They cut off the executive from the line organization and the line organization from the executive." Further, "A strong central staff will find something to do and will eventually decide that what it wants to do is sufficiently important that it justifies interfering with what somebody else wants to do."

Staff groups in looking for ways to apply their specialty often take away the functions that line management has to perform. An example is the story of Work Simplification, an effective performance improvement tool that was the forerunner of the current process improvement initiatives.

Work Simplification was a system that was developed in the '30s by Allan Mogensen. This program taught first-line supervisors the techniques of improving work systems and workflow. It also taught their managers and top executives how to support the improvements suggested by the supervisors. Of course, this is the same program that people like Juran and Deming took and added statistical analyses to and presented as a new idea in the '80s.

The staff people rediscovered Work Simplification in the '60s. They took over the implementation of this approach under various other names. The result was not the same as before because the line management did not feel that they had direct accountability to produce results. Before, line managers and supervisors were improving their own work, the work for which they were accountable. But now the staff undertook a number of corporate issues for which line management had no direct accountability. Again staff took away functions from line management, added irrelevant subject, and made a mockery of an effective approach to management.

IMPROVING LINE-STAFF RELATIONSHIPS

There is no magic pill that will make this problem go away. It has grown insidiously over a long time and is firmly entrenched in most organizations. Our advice to top management is to begin again to attend to the basics by re-establishing the accountabilities that rightly belong to the line organization and by reinforcing the role of staff groups as expert advisors and consultants. The place to start is to define the accountabilities that should clearly establish the role each is to play. The definitions we recommend are:

"Line managers and supervisors are accountable for all acts, activities, performance, morale, safety, training, etc-in other words, everything-of all those people who report to those managers and supervisors and only those people."

"Through the quality and persuasiveness of their expert advice and counsel, staff groups are accountable for improving line managers ability to manage and supervise."

These are both straightforward definitions, which clearly identify line management as the key players in carrying out the company's business and staff departments as those who function in the background to provide the needed services and expertise. The ideal relationship can be illustrated by a line manager and a staff person sitting across the table from one another, assertively laying out their positions on the problem at hand. Staff people are accountable for being persuasive —-to "sell" their recommendations through expert knowledge, current facts and information, and a logical presentation of their case. Too many staff people have the knowledge but cannot persuade. The real horror story, however, is the reverse-staff people who are very persuasive but don't know what they're talking about.

Given their time across the table from each other, it is the line manager's decision whether or not to accept the advice offered. Whether accepted or not, the manager is still accountable for the consequences. If accepted, the staff person is accountable for the quality and effectiveness of the advice given; if not accepted, the staff person is accountable for lack of persuasiveness. In no way should staff people be accountable for the end results that are produced in a line department. Similarly, line managers are accountable for those end results regardless of the success or failure of the staff person's advice or service.

Top management would do well to begin now to reeducate both line and staff groups as to their respective accountabilities. Problems that arise in these relationships are often the result of ignorance on the part of both line and staff groups. In our management seminars, we ask the participants how many of them have ever been exposed to a detailed discussion of line-staff relationships and the accountabilities of each. Rarely in a group of twenty managers, many with years of experience in management, do more than one or two hands go up. Education and awareness is the logical place to start.

The sad story of staff groups can be added to our discussion in Chapter Two, The Obstacles to Greatness. A quick survey of the executives of today's major companies will reveal that many of them reached their positions through the staff route. Most CEOs are not products of their operating environments, have not come up through the ranks, and too often are elevated to their position because of their expertise in financial or other staff disciplines. Being a product of a staff function, CEOs tend to seek advice from like kinds - other people in staff functions. They are the most likely source to be tapped by the CEO to provide solutions to problems with which they have little firsthand experience.

Relations between staff and operating people, even at the executive level, are often strained and distant, an uneasy truce at best. Why? Simply because respect for organizational and managerial intellect and ability is not bestowed on the "doers" in the organization-the manufacturing managers, engineers, and others who run the place, day by day. These experienced operating people are considered to be "in the here and now" with little or no ability to look beyond getting today's work done today.

It's safe to predict, therefore, that the greed mongers, the bean counters, and the "deus ex machina" leaders of tomorrow will come from the ranks of the power brokers of today. Until organizations learn to mine the riches that exist in the collective wisdom and experience of their operating personnel-the people and the departments for whom the rest of the organization should exist-the relentless devastation of organizations and their human resources will continue.

CHAPTER EIGHT

TOP EXECUTIVES: EXTERNAL MANAGEMENT

We have said earlier that we chose the title of our book "Managing Without the CEO" not because we don't recognize the difficulty of a CEO's job but because we are convinced that the true internal management of an organization must be performed by middle managers and not by the CEO. The CEO, along with other top executives, should manage the critical external issues. The internal affairs should be managed by capable middle mangers, equipped with the appropriate skills and knowledge(s) discussed in earlier chapters.

Top executives by definition occupy the highest management level in the organization. They include Chairman of the Board, Chief Executive Officer (CEO), and other key positions such as Chief Operating Officer (COO), Chief Financial Officer (CFO), and Chief Legal Officer (CLO). Each organization must identify for itself which positions belong to the top executive group since every firm operates differently. However, the top executive positions should not be determined by title alone or for political reasons.

The primary job of top management is to ensure the long-term growth and perpetuation of the organization. Top management should accomplish this by devoting upwards of 75 percent of their time on matters external to the day-by-day operations of the company. Often when we ask managers and supervisors what their top executives spend their time on, they respond, "golf, travel junkets, and three-martini lunches." Our response is "Terrific, as long as they're golfing, traveling, and dining with the right people for the right purposes."

External management, then, is the primary job of

the top executives. It covers two main functions: the entrepreneurial function and the customer, public, and government relations functions.

ENTREPRENEURIAL FUNCTION

The dictionary defines an entrepreneur as "a person who organizes and directs a business undertaking, assuming the risk for the sake of profit." In an organization there must be only one source of true entrepreneurship. When too many people in one organization act as entrepreneurs, the result is often indecision and chaos. Conflicting directions ultimately will weaken the organization.

It is fashionable these days to think of all employees as entrepreneurs. That concept is nothing short of a fantasy. The perception evolved from a movement in the '80s toward intrapreneurship. The main premise of this concept was that employees at all levels of the organization are capable of making risk-taking decisions and coming up with innovative ways to improve products and performance. The example often used is the creation of Post-its by an employee at 3M.

Whatever the merit of intraprenuership, it is far removed from the entrepreneurship required of top executives. At this organizational level, decisions made today are based on visions of the future. And these decisions, costing perhaps millions of today's dollars, will determine not only the future success but also the very survival of the company. To have a vision of the future, to plan and initiate innovations based on that vision, and have the courage to invest huge amounts of current resources to it are the fundamentals of entrepreneurship. And few have the talent and courage to do it consistently well.

Identifying the traits that a successful entrepreneur must possess is difficult at best. There is no instrument or index that can predict with validity whether becoming a successful entrepreneur is in anyone's future. Whenever writers have tried to identify the unique characteristics of an entrepreneur, they have ended up with a collection of conflicting attributes. There are simply too many different and varied factors in making a person an entrepreneur. It is not possible to find a consistent pattern around which an effective training program for entrepreneurs can be developed. Those who try often confuse entrepreneurship with leadership, proving that they don't understand either concept.

True entrepreneurship cannot be taught. It is a rare combination of the right circumstances: environment, family up bringing, experiential learning, special education (not necessarily formal schooling), and a set of uncontrollable genetic factors, sprinkled liberally with luck. Being in the right place at the right time with the right product surrounded by the right people certainly doesn't hurt. There is no way anyone can teach or provide this combination of factors. Nature and chance create entrepreneurs, and enough of them emerge that we don't need to have deep concerns about creating clones.

Paul Reichmann, a real estate entrepreneur, is an excellent example of the unusual attributes it takes to make a person an entrepreneur. Reichmann had Talmudic instructions for more than five years. He was actually qualified to become a rabbi, but instead, he followed his entrepreneurial instincts and built one of the world's largest real estate empires. Mr. Reichmann, the epitome of entrepreneurship, is proof-positive that the entrepreneurial part of a CEO's make-up is mostly instinctive rather than achieved by education or training. Thousands of MBAs are awarded each year in this country, but only a small percentage of those graduates ever become successful entrepreneurs.

Consider the fact that shortly after the fall of Communism, a group of entrepreneurs emerged in Russia, without training or formal business skills. Russians still don't fully understand capitalism, organizational structure, or management, yet they have had some significant successes with the native born entrepreneurs. Most of the Russian entrepreneurs still lack business skills, but they are very effective in "risk taking and profit making."

As an entrepreneur, a CEO must make the final decisions on issues such as:

1. Capital Provisions: should the organization borrow money, issue stocks, offer bonds or provide the needed capital through internal cash flow and internal growth?

2. Marketing: should the organization expand the market to other regions, other countries?

3. Product Development: should the organization develop new products, improve existing ones, or purchase other companies with the targeted products already developed?

4. Financial/Growth/Future: should the organization expand by purchasing other companies, merge for growth, or sell to the highest bidder?

We are not suggesting that a CEO make all these decisions alone. An effective CEO consults with key executives and managers and analyzes all available options. But there is no one to share the accountability; the final accountability for entrepreneurship rests solely with the CEO.

The second major accountability of top executive is the continual development of a series of relations: customer relations, public relations, and government relations.

CUSTOMER RELATIONS

There are basically two kinds of customers for the top executives to consider: 1) shareholders and bondholders and 2) major customers of the products or services the organization provides. Neither group is interested in hearing about the present and future of the company from anybody but the top executives.

Shareholders must be kept informed and managed. By nature, shareholders are capricious. For many their loyalty is to the growth of stock prices and increase in dividends. Investors are also demanding and often downright greedy. The CEO must demonstrate to them that it is best for the shareholders to maintain a long- term outlook in the organization. Short-term values create turmoil and problems for the equilibrium of the organization. Organizational equilibrium demands that the shareholders, the organization, the employees, and the public be treated as equal partners for the long- term success of the company. Short-term profits cause critical long-term results for the organization.

When a CEO tries to communicate the value of long-term investment as a reason for stockholders to stay the course, the shareholders with no loyalty to the organization often turn deaf ears, choosing rather to sell their shares. This may be a blessing in disguise by ridding the company of a negative influence. The remaining shareholders will show stronger support for the future of the organization and its top executives.

Catering to the short-term mindset of stockholders and investors may well be a prescription for disaster. Frederick F. Reichheld (*The Loyalty Effect*) writes "It is management's over-attentiveness to the demands of these short-term investors that is stalling growth at many companies." Some CEOs have unwittingly become advocates for the shareholders to the detriment of the future growth of the company. Other CEOs have wittingly become advocates for shareholders, including themselves, as exemplified by the current trend to float IPOs. In the initial offering, the opening stock price immediately skyrockets, the first-in-line investors (who bought at the opening price) sell their shares, the stock price tumbles, and the rest of the investors are the losers.

This, in the minds of some, is entrepreneurship. However, caveat emptor should be the motto of shareholders and investors as it is in buying any product or commodity. Let the buyer beware. To us, it's much the same as the telemarketing scams which have put a number of "entrepreneurs" where they belong-cooling their heels in jail.

Major customers are also a critical group with whom top executives should be in regular contact. These contacts should not be for purposes of selling products or services but for the purpose of continually selling the company as the best place for the customers to do business. Developing lasting relationships with the top management of major customers should not be relegated to staff people, public relations departments, middle managers, or sales people. CEO's want to talk to CEOs when major decisions or commitments of capital are to be made. And the first contacts are likely to be between CEOs who have established a solid business-and often personal/social-relationship.

No example is more pertinent than the case of Louis V. Gerstner, Chairman and CEO of IBM. When Mr. Gerstner took over the company, IBM was experiencing critical financial problems due to years of mismanagement. The majority of management "gurus," at the time doubted that Mr. Gerstner could improve IBM's situation. They asked themselves "What does he know about computers?"

Tom Peters (USA Today, March 29, 1993) expressed his doubt: "What's my bet? He [Gerstner] has only a 40% chance of pulling off something significant. They [Wall Street people] want it all. They want this tough S.O.B. who can shape up the troops, can weed out bad assets. But in the back of their minds is this dream that by 1998 we'll have a new IBM that shines like the old. It's nutty."

Well, "nutty" or not, Mr. Gerstner's 40 percent chance given by Tom Peters became 100 percent. He may not have recreated the same old IBM, but he has a new one which is as good. Even the Wall Street manipulators are happy with him. Tom Peters doubted in vain.

Steve Jobs, then chairman of NeXt Computer commented, "If G. [Gestner] can bring out the technical talent already in that company and find the right people to trust, he might do fine. But how will he know who [sic] to trust?"

Most probably Mr. Jobs was thinking of his own predicament with John Scully when Mr. Scully ousted him from Apple Computers. Mr. Jobs had trusted Scully only to be betrayed by him and then Scully single-handedly ruined the future of a great organization. He was so enamored with the concept of the "Virtual Organization" that he lost sight of the real organization. Andrew Grove, Chairman of Intel, called the virtual organization "a business buzz phrase that's meaningless. It's appetizing but you get nothing out of it."

Among all the predictors of Mr. Gestner's future, only Warren Bennis assessed the situation correctly. "People wonder if he's technologically literate," maintained Bennis. "Lou has something even more important. That's business literacy. He understands what's needed at IBM. And that's not technological virtuosity. He has a great capacity to pick terrific people."

Mr. Bennis understood the role of a CEO well. He knew that a CEO need not have "technological virtuosity." But a CEO must have a great deal of "business literacy." We fully support Bennis' concept of what constitutes an effective CEO.

Gerstner quickly proved that knowing a great deal about computers was not going to solve IBM's problems. He left that to the engineers and the technicians, those with the "technological virtuosity." Being an effective CEO does not depend on detailed knowledge of either the products or the services of the company. On the contrary, an effective CEO must, above all, be knowledgeable in entrepreneurship and customer relations. Mr. Gerstner's meetings with IBM's major customers not only cemented the existing business but also provided input and direction for future products. Additionally, it created a positive word-of-mouth reputation among IBM's clients.

His effective performance in this area allowed IBM to take away several major accounts from its competitors like Tandem, Hewlett-Packard, Oracle, Unisys, Anderson Consulting, Digital Equipment, NCR, and Apple.

Gerstner also met often with major investors, not only to listen to their concerns, but also to keep them informed of IBM's present and future plans. This networking brought results across the board. Employment was steady after the initial downsizing. IBM moved in a winning direction. The communities in which IBM was active gained continuous economic support from IBM payroll and taxes, and the investors were rewarded. Mr. Gerstner did an extraordinary job in a relatively short period of time. And what he did, almost step by step, has been defined for so many years in our seminars, and now, in this book, as a model for other CEOs.

PUBLIC RELATIONS

A CEO's public relation job demands involvement with the community in which the organization is located. The public must regularly hear about the values the organization adds to the lives of the community and to the public in general. When a company contributes to a community activity (time, money, or both) that fact should come to light through activities by the senior executives of the company and not just by the efforts of the public relations staff. While gifts or money are the favored approaches, public relations activities tend to be more effective when they involve a sacrifice of time devoted by the top executives. When a CEO serves on the board of some community organization free of charge or donates time to a charitable cause, he or she earns the respect of the entire community. And a good public relations department makes sure that this type of top management activity is well publicized.

At times CEOs perform very poorly in their public relations function. Some CEOs, such as Michael Eisner, CEO of Walt Disney World, exemplifies this failing. In an interview with Ronald Grover, the Bureau Chief of Business Week (August 14, 1997) in response to Mr. Grover's question about the problems with Disney's animation unit, Mr. Eisner's response was a monotonous "nothing is wrong." The problem, he maintained was that people just don't understand that business. His strategy was to move to other issues that were not raised in the interview.

Following is a portion of the interchange between Mr. Grover and Mr. Eisner (remember Mr. Eisner is trying to improve the image of Disney World by giving an interview in an important business magazine):

Grover: "Box office receipts have been going down since Lion King, and that can't be a good trend for sustaining that strategy. Can it?"

Eisner: "The trend is just fine."

Grover: "What was the problem with Insane Clown Posse [a hard core rap album, 100,000 copies of which were withdrawn]. How did that one slip through the cracks?"

Eisner: "Has Business Week ever made a mistake?"

Grover: "Can we discuss the problem of ABC?"

Eisner: "ABC is not a problem."

Investors and the general public may not understand the nature of Mr. Eisner's business but they do understand the fiasco in hiring Mr. Ovitz and then firing him after a few months and paying him $100 million from the earnings of the company. Then they recall the suit for $250 million by Mr. Jefferson Katzenberg against Walt Disney World that eventually was settled out of court for millions of dollars from the earnings of the company.

Mr. Eisner, as a CEO, has not done well in other aspects either. For example, his entrepreneurial activity in Euro Disney in France was a mistake. Had it not been for a half a billion dollars in investment by Prince Alwaleed of Saudi Arabia, the European venture would have been in bankruptcy by now.

The tendency in discussing top management's role in public relations is to focus on large companies with high-profile CEOs who often adorn the covers of mainstream business publications. However, CEOs, presidents, and owners of medium and small organizations also need to be heavily involved in the public and community activities that provide the exposure their business needs.

How small and medium-sized organizations can benefit enormously by the public relations efforts of top management is illustrated by our work with the public library in South Pasadena, CA. In 1990, the South Pasadena Public Library (SOPA) was being managed in the traditional way. The Library Director was primarily concerned with internal, day-to-day, operations and with state and national association activities. She was well known among other library directors and was considered a knowledgeable, articulate representative of the profession. Circulation of library materials was considered adequate for the size of the library, as was the number of registered borrowers and patrons. Membership in the Friends of the Library, a community support group, was relatively low and volunteer hours were limited.

During that year, the library director resigned and her replacement was hired. We had the opportunity to work with the new director in her previous middle management positions and were now in a position to assist in her transition to top management. She began her tenure at SOPA with two primary goals: to develop her management staff to handle daily operations, and to get the community leadership, city council, and citizens more aware of, and involved in, library functions. The first goal had to precede the second. Without solid internal management, it is nearly impossible to carry out successful external management.

During her second and subsequent years, the director estimated that nearly seventy-five percent of her time was spent on external activities. These included attendance at all city council meetings and functions, civic affairs of every imaginable kind, speeches to local organizations, consulting with the Friends groups to increase membership and involvement, recruiting and organizing volunteers, applying for grants, donating time to local charitable organizations, and responding personally to every library donor. Her internal activities were devoted primarily to staff development and getting the right people in the right jobs. She also budgeted time to be on the floor, interacting with patrons and staff members.

It was during this period that budget cuts and downsizing became the order of the day. Other library systems in California and elsewhere were cutting staff, reducing hours, offering fewer services, and buying far fewer library books and materials. In the city of South Pasadena, however, under the leadership of the director, the citizens passed a Library Parcel Tax, guaranteeing a protected funding increase for the next five years. Of the many that tried during 1995, only three cities in California succeeded in passing such a tax. There is no question that the director's external activities and skills were the primary contributors to that success.

The performance of the library itself is also testimony to the value of effective external management. Comparing 1990 to 1996, registered borrowers increased 141 percent; people using the library by 33 percent; revenues by 654 percent; circulation by 50 percent; reference questions by 70 percent; and volunteer hours by 121 percent. All of this was managed with an increase in staffing of only 1.5 positions in a six-year period. Clearly the library had become what all libraries should be-a community asset.

Ask the director and she'll say that it's because of her great staff, good community leadership, and wonderful people. Ask us and we'll tell you she's much too modest. None of it would have happened without her understanding of external management principles and her tireless efforts to carry them out.

GOVERNMENT RELATIONS

Good government relations are more important now then they have ever been. Over the past few decades, the federal government primarily has intruded into almost every facet of business activities. Enormous amounts of resources are devoted to complying with an ever-increasing number of rules and regulations. The increased paperwork generated must surely deplete the timber that the Environmental Protection Agency is trying diligently to save.

Perhaps in a negative way, government intrusion illustrates just how important it is for top management to be continuously involved in what's going on in Washington, in state capitals, and in city council boardrooms. The current state of affairs may well be a direct result of a lack of executive attention to this critical function. Contributing to political campaigns is not enough and having paid lobbyists is not enough. Senior executives must be involved proactively in interacting with governmental officials and agencies at all levels and on a continuous basis. Several companies that have been bailed out by governmental action will attest to the fact that it is good idea to not only be a presence in the halls of Congress but to maintain a part-time residence in Georgetown.

While CEOs bewail the fact that increased government intrusion has severely hampered their companies' growth, there are those among them that have directly contributed to a more active governmental role. In some instances, CEOs and other top executives have tried to obtain special advantages for themselves or their organizations or have carried out illegal or unethical behavior, often for personal gains. Throughout the last decade, a small but significant number of organizations have suffered huge penalties, and top executives punished severely for such actions.

Among them are Mr. Miscall Moneys, co-founder and CEO of Farmer, Inc., who received a twenty-year jail sentence and a $1 million dollar fine for embezzlement and for issuing phony financial statements. Warner-Lambert was fined $10 million for hiding certain manufacturing processes from the FDA.

The Tenet Company had to pay more than $500 million to settle charges and plead guilty to eight criminal counts. The payments went to the government, the insurance companies, doctors, patients, and a large number of lawyers. Archer Daniel Midland pled guilty to conspiring with competitors to set prices and was assessed a fine of $100 million. We count the culprits in these organizations among the greed mongers and the bean counters who too often reside on mahogany row.

As abhorrent as corruption is, in business or elsewhere, it is compounded by the backlash it produces. Not only do customers, shareholders, investors, and employees shun such corrupt organizations, but also all other companies suffer from the preventives put in place by government agencies. As in all other facets of society, major missteps by a few have resulted in punishing restrictions placed on the many. The current trend toward legislative control of business practices in the marketplace and management practices within the workplace can be laid at the feet of those few top executives who willingly subverted the rules of social behavior and common decency or turned a blind eye when others in their organizations did.

Keeping government out of the workplace is often as simple as not giving them a reason to enter in the first place.

A CEO's job is to influence the influencers. And any CEO who takes government lightly as an influencer does so at his or her peril.

TOP EXECUTIVES ROLE IN INTERNAL MANAGEMENT

While internal management should be the purview of middle management, should top management get involved? Since middle managers report to executives and thus take directions from them, it is obvious that top management plays a critical role in managing the organization internally. Among top management's responsibilities is clearly communicating the mission and direction of the organization and determining the broad policies and procedures through which that mission is to be realized. Of equal importance, but rarely done well, is communicating and orchestrating shifts in the direction and modification in the mission as changes in the business environment so often demand. The speed with which these changes occur and the company's agility to adapt quickly make this responsibility particularly difficult. Many companies who fail to keep up with change do so, not because the need and the means to change were not identified in time, but because the process of change was not well planned and communicated to those who had to implement it. Internal managers cannot respond effectively if external managers fail to provide the direction and the resources to do so.

A second role of top management is to ensure that internal management is working well according to the established mission and direction. Mission and vision statements hung ceremoniously on every wall in the organization do little but enhance the esthetics of the environment. Such statements are glowing tributes to the ambitions of the organization but are much too vague to have little beyond public relations value. Mission statements must be translated into operating plans that clearly describe the overall principles, policies, processes, and resources required to move the company steadily toward the mission. A major part of the operating plan should be a set of organizational objectives determined by top management and cascaded down through the management structure. Accountability for performance related to each objective should be firmly established.

There are four types of objectives that should be included in the operating business plan:

1. Maintenance Objectives: objectives pertaining to those parts of the business that are performing well and need to keep performing that way. Improvements may not be possible or expected. Often organizations ignore this type of objective because maintaining existing levels of performance is perceived as a "given." Why prepare objectives if there is to be no improvement? The answer is simple. We often fail to maintain what we have because our efforts are driven entirely by what must be improved. Maintaining existing accounts is as important as getting new ones.

    A second reason that maintenance objectives are ignored is that most managers are weaned on problem solving. Given the opportunity they will solve problems, even if the benefits of the solution are far less than the cost of solving the problem. It doesn't take long for a new supervisor to realize that the path to middle management is through problem solving. No one got promoted by meeting maintenance objectives. However, it is not uncommon for managers to be fired because they did not maintain a level of performance in key areas in which maintenance was all that was required. Maintenance objectives are every bit as important, if not as glamorous, as improvement objectives.

2. Improvement Objectives: objectives to hone existing operations and processes that may be func-

tioning adequately but with improvement would significantly improve the pay-off from such functions. Generally, the number of improvement objectives should be limited to a critical few, perhaps no more than three or four. If there are too many performance objectives, the efforts will be diluted to the extent that none of them will be fully exploited.

3. Problem Solving Objectives: objectives focused on finding ways to solve specific problems currently facing the organization. As with improvement objectives, they should be few in number and relate to problems which are clearly affecting the company's overall performance. The objective at this stage should focus on finding the solutions, conducting a cost-benefit analysis, and providing a preliminary plan of implementation. The concept at this stage is to concentrate on solutions and recommending actions.

4. New Objectives: objectives related to new ideas, innovations, studies, and other approaches that would bring new directions and fresh ideas into the organization.

This operating plan must be discussed in detail with middle managers so that they can adapt it to their own departments. Each layer of management must be accountable for the various objectives of the organization and a plan for periodic upward reviews and modifications must be put in place. The working plan will allow the top management to receive updated feedback from their managers directly. These feedback sessions must not be done solely via a series of perfunctory reports or routine items on staff meeting agendas. There must also be at least quarterly face-to-face follow-up meetings so that proper adjustments can be made.

Among the reasons for recommending face-to-face follow-up meetings between top management and their managers highlights another internal role for top management. Top management is accountable for training and developing mangers just as supervisors and managers are accountable for developing their subordinates. Unfortunately, most executives pay little attention to this important part of their jobs, assuming that managers wouldn't have their jobs unless they already knew how to do them or that the training department will take care of management training. The net result has been that managers receive training on just about everything except managing. At best, the training that managers receive is a harmless collection of generic skills and concepts or personal development theories that have little to do with their jobs. At worst, management-training programs are an enormous waste of time and money and, at times, can be downright destructive to individuals and to the organizations.

Top management too often heeds the advice of their training departments and high-priced consultants who peddle the latest management theories derived from university studies or from best-selling books. Wilderness training and the "Seven Habits" are the most recent fads that are draining the training budgets. Sensitivity Training-echoes of the past-is now becoming the remedy of choice for anyone who looks sideways at another employee.

Irrelevancies and contradictions abound in these types of management programs. Top management's first priority is developing managers as managers. Perhaps then they can afford to waste a few extra dollars on personal homilies and tree climbing.

A Balloon Waiting to be Burst? Pseudomanagement Training, by Stephen Williams, is a study of management training in the U.K. Mr. Williams could have written almost the same words about U.S. management training theories. He writes, "There is a tremendous stress on teamwork, and welding a team together. Are you a 'Mover,' a 'Shaper,' or a 'Plant?' Hidden strengths and weaknesses are revealed, and personalities analyzed. Is one a control freak or a sycophant? It is no use disagreeing about the diagnosis because that's just a symptom of repression and refusal to face the truth about yourself. It's all close to group therapy. There are appeals to Zen and the Tao. But what has all this got to do with actual management?"

Williams goes on to write, "If this were just a case of waste, fashionable fads, and follies, then it would be a little sad but only too familiar. In reality it is worse than that. Many young executives are practical and dedicated men and women who want to do their jobs well and advance their careers. But instead they are being palmed off with trendy hokum which may lull them into believing they have learned something when they have not."

Williams maintains that there is no follow-up and that management faces the same problems after training that they did before training. Dr. James Cook, author of Management Training: Don't Waste Your Money, states that not only must there be a follow up for management training, but there must also be considerable time spent before the actual training to prepare the participants and establish the management tasks that require the use of skills taught in the program. First and foremost, however, before follow-up even becomes an issue, the skills and concepts taught in the classroom must be above all else relevant, applicable to the job of managing, and be consistent with the environment in which the training is to be applied. The last thing any organization should want is on-the-job follow-up of irrelevant training.

Training in Motorola is a good example of taking too much time for the training activity without sufficient time and effort on the follow-up and implementation of skills learned. Motorola has spent more than $126 million a year on Total Quality Management training. All employees were required to attend at least forty hours of training per year. Early results were impressive. Their Six-Sigma approach earned them the coveted Malcom Baldridge National Quality Award and a whirlwind of beneficial public relations. Staff managers were speakers in every gathering and every conference. Organizations by the droves were sending their staff groups and teams to benchmark Motorola. Six-Sigma was the magic pill that was going to propel companies to great heights in the millennium. Other companies such as Allied and General Electric profited considerably from their application of the Six-Sigma quality program.

The Achilles' heel of Total Quality Management and Six-Sigma, however, was the total neglect of the training and involvement of middle managers in the implementation of these initiatives. Companies forgot that major change must be managed into the organization. It will not occur simply because top management says it will or because other organizations have apparently been successful or because millions of training dollars have been spent. What they forgot to do was to prepare managers in how to manage in this new environment. All the statistical analysis in the world is not going to produce change unless management makes it happen. While the battle cry of TQM was to get top management involved, to get them to "walk the talk," the effort while commendable was completely misguided. The key players in the implementation of any new company-wide initiatives are not the top executives. The key players are the internal managers who are accountable for the on-the-floor day-by-day operations where the changes must occur.

Top management's efforts should have been directed toward doing what they get paid to do-preparing their middle managers to manage TQM or Six Sigma or any major change effort into their organizations. Motorola had indicated that by the year 2000 they would be spending more than $600 million on training. We certainly hope a significant portion of that budget is allocated to top management for the training and development of their managers.

An outstanding model of a CEO who works hard to develop managers is Mr. Jack Welch, CEO of General Electric. Each management-training group is handpicked for a two-week management-training program. Mr. Welch always meets them and spends more than half a day discussing management concepts and principles. All the courses in management training curriculum are chosen to support and facilitate the key objectives of General Electric, as expressed by the operating units, rather than by staff functions.

As opposed to Motorola's approach, GE provides a great deal of follow-up after the training. Mr. Welch's yearly talk at the conference with his top five hundred executives is videotaped and copies are given to each attendee to facilitate holding meetings with his or her management group. In turn the managers hold discussions with their people until the message is cascaded down to everyone. This unity of purpose and open communication is one of Mr. Welch's key successes in taking a $21 billion company in 1981 to greater heights today.

Mr. Welch's approach epitomizes Peter Drucker's concept of what an organization can achieve. Drucker sums it up in saying, "The purpose of an organization is to enable ordinary people to do extraordinary things." In Drucker's vocabulary, Mr. Welch has gone well beyond the concept by not only developing extraordinary people, but also by developing an extraordinary organization. Our admiration for Mr. Welch is in large part because of his extraordinary efforts to develop his management team.

Another success story is exemplified by Siemens, which uses one of the most interesting approaches in developing managers. Instead of having a classroom with instructors talking theory, managers are given real operating problems to solve. They work together in the analysis of the problems and in preparing recommendations. Because of the relevancy of the training, Siemens has reduced their dependency on outside consultants and other related classroom costs, saving the company $11 million from its inception until now (USA Today, November 15, 1999).

ISSUES FOR CEOS AND TOP MANAGEMENT

CEOs and top management are at a crossroads. They can continue the pernicious trend of the last ten to fifteen years, or actively attempt to make their organizations the center of value in this country. If CEOs and top management continue to utilize organizations as money-making machines from which they can line their pockets and those of their stockholders, greed will continue to be the force that drives many organizations. The business community and its employees will then be saddled with an employment market with a huge gap between those few in highly technical jobs and the tens-of-millions of hamburger makers, machine baby-sitters, and welfare recipients.

Confidence in the ability of top management to care for all the stakeholders is at its lowest point in decades. According to the 1998-99 Hay Employee Attitudes study the confidence of middle managers, professional and technical staff, and clerical support regarding the ability of top management has been reduced significantly. The greatest percentage of decrease is among the clerical and middle managers. There was very little change in the attitude of the hourly workers because they didn't have much confidence in the first place.

Our fear is that this kind of a business environment will give rise to a corps of militant white color workers, the likes of which we have not seen since the 1930s. In this crucial time of decision, CEOs and top management play the pivotal role. They can, if they choose, change the trend before it's too late.

In order to change this trend CEOs and top management, in addition to performing their described functions, must take actions in the following areas: compensation, training, and line management trust.

Compensation

Compensation packages for the CEOs of major companies have become outrageous, unfair, unethical, and the cause of problems yet to come. Some CEOs receive, as we have indicated before, 419 times the salary of the average paycheck in the organization-not 419 times of the lowest paid person, but 419 time the average pay. The result? A major class separation and deep-seeded negative feelings among almost all levels within an organization.

Such outrageous compensation ratios must be reduced quickly and drastically. Peter Drucker in an interview with Robert Lenzner and Stephen S. Johnson for Forbes Magazine (March 10, 1997) said: "In the next economic downturn there will be an outbreak of bitterness and contempt for the super-corporate chieftains who pay themselves millions." We believe that the reaction will be more than "bitterness and contempt," since CEOs have paid themselves billions, not millions in the last three years.

It is extravagant for Michael D. Eisner to receive over $590 million in one year on his stock options alone, plus his salary, benefits, and ad nauseam. In 1996, Business Week named Eisner the worst CEO (for the third straight year) based on return to shareholders. Disney is lucky to have a few highly creative people to meet the insatiable desire for entertainment throughout the world. Otherwise Disney, with its hyped status and arrogant style of management, would not be a successful company.

Standard accounting practices have not helped these situations. When most of a CEO's compensation is through stock options, the amount does not affect the financial statement of the organization. However, when employees (whether they are mission workers, supervisors, or managers) get a $1 an hour raise, the amount is reflected on the financial statement, reducing the net profit. Shareholders, familiar with this practice, are therefore willing to give stock options to CEOs, but they criticize CEOs if labor costs increase and net profits decrease.

The consequence of this type of action is that employees have begun to resent top management. They view top management as a protected species. Opportunistic lawyers and CPAs have devised golden parachutes and poison pills, providing enormous sums of money to executives with little relationship to any contributions to their companies. Resentment of the protected species has a ripple effect well beyond specific companies and their employees. The general perception of business as a socio-economic institution becomes linked again to the flimflam man, the shylock, and the confidence game.

To be sure, executives deserve top dollar when their performance warrants it. But so does everybody else in the organization. We're not talking about a re-distribution of wealth. We're simply talking about a fair shake for everybody. If stock options are a way of compensation, it is only fair that everyone in the organization should be eligible after a reasonable period of service, and we're happy to see that some organizations have implemented such a plan. The next step is to make the parachutes golden for everybody, given equity relative to one's contribution to the organization. How to pay for it? Reduce the obscene amounts given to top management and use those funds to compensate those who do the work that produces that income to begin with.

We are not suggesting that every CEO must follow the example of John Tu and David Sun, co-founders of Kingston Technology, who sold 80 percent of their company for $1.5 billion, and gave $40 million in employee bonuses with another $60 million slated for employee education and other employee programs. The CEOs who are greed mongers or bean counters will not even understand the actions of Mr. Tu and Mr. Sun. They couldn't comprehend a philosophy that says "We want to show you that we can run a company by putting the people first-and not treating them just as expenses."

We don't even suggest that every CEO must act as John Lauer. When he agreed to become the CEO of Oglebay Norton Mr. Lauer refused to accept a salary, and he paid $1 million of his own money for his shares of company stocks. Upon insistence of the board, he agreed to receive a bonus if the company met certain financial goals.

Neither do we expect too many CEOs to follow the concepts of S. Robert Levine, President, and Craig R. Benson, Chairman, of Cabletron, who both draw annual salaries of $52,000. In all, 420 out of 4,900 employees earn more than the President and the Chairman. Their low top executive salaries are right in tune with their frugal corporate culture. There are no plush offices or even fancy conference rooms. Everyone has a metal desk in a Spartan office. Following the advice of Townsend (Up the Organization), there are no chairs in their conference rooms so managers can finish their meetings as quickly as possible. There are also no first-class airline tickets, no plush hotel rooms or suites, and the maximum daily meal allowance is $35.

Business Week quotes Paul R. Duncan, chief financial officer of Reebok and a Cabletron director, referring to these pioneering CEOs, as saying "They march to a different drummer." We like the music of that drummer very much, and we hope that other CEOs will learn a few critical lessons from Levine and Benson. They need not try to match Levine's and Benson's extremely low salaries, but they could implement some of their ideas and philosophies. "Those guys are driven by a need to be efficient, fast, and lean," says Duncan, "and they are setting an example for the rest of the company's employees."

Some executives will consider Tu and Sun, Lauer, and Levine and Benson to be naive, crazy, or egocentric. The same executives most probably will not read this book or, if they do, will not understand it, or, if they understand it, will probably think we're naive, crazy, or egocentric. In reality, the CEOs who will read and appreciate this book are those who want to build an effective organization in this country. They want to provide meaningful work and commensurate compensation for the employees, great products or services for their customers, a reasonable return for the investors, and support for the communities in which they live and work.

We recommend that CEOs follow Jack Welch's approach in General Electric Co. where he has included more than 27,000 of the employees in the stock option plan. His stock option plan is not a seniority-based plan, but a performance-based plan. We hope to see the day that GE will include all workers on this plan. Bill Gates and his top management team at Microsoft, despite their current antitrust rift with the Justice Department, are well known for providing outstanding compensation and benefit packages to all levels of the organization.

We believe the most practical approach would be to share some of the earnings with all the employees, as Intel Corp. did in 1997 when they shared $800 million with the employees. Even the entry-level worker who started at $25,000 per year received $8,000 extra in shared earnings. We believe Mr. Craig Barrett, then the Chief Operating Officer of Intel, was correct when he said, "We think it's also been a phenomenal benefit to our shareholders by motivating our employees to do the best possible job they can for our shareholders and our customers."

The Training Fantasy

Corporate America spends more than $60 billion on training. When you figure in the salary and the benefits of those who are being trained, the cost actually amounts to a staggering $280 billion-more than is spent on education in the fifty states and the District of Columbia. The question: what kind of results are we getting for our money? The answer: a conservative estimate is that more than half of the cost for training and development is a total waste of resources.

While the reasons are many and varied, a significant amount of the waste is directly attributable to top management's directives to conduct enormously expensive training programs, company-wide, with little or no basis for predicting that the training will have any organizational benefit. As described in chapter two, "The Obstacles to Greatness," CEOs and executives are highly susceptible to the smooth-talking academic theorists or best-selling author-of-the-month. Millions of training dollars are spent on company-wide initiatives with little evidence that the training will provide any return for the resources expended. Pity the poor executive who authorizes that kind of money for new machinery without first going through a rigorous cost-return analysis and testing to validate its worth.

A large telecommunications company recently discontinued company-wide training on the "Seven Habits" with the explanation that it was too costly to continue. Since the company continues to do very well financially, a likely translation of the explanation is that there is no commensurate value for the dollars spent.

Another current example of training that is mandated by top management in many organizations is wilderness training. By climbing mountains, sliding down ropes, and jumping into the arms of co-workers to show trust and allegiance, managers are supposed to learn to manage better. Those who have gone through the program and said they liked it also admitted they might be equating the novelty, the excitement and the fresh air with a relevant learning experience.

There's an axiom in training that says, "People learn by doing that which they are doing." It basically means that by sliding down ropes people learn how to slide down ropes. The quantum leap that has to be made is that sliding down a rope and falling off a tree stump is transferable to other things that need to be learned and dealt with in the organization. If it was true that one learning experience can teach us another, we would not have to build expensive simulators and training programs to train pilots how to fly. They could transfer their ability in driving a car over to flying. How many people, we wonder, would be willing to fly with a pilot who has only been trained to drive a car?

In its cover story of August 19, 1996, USA Today reported that the cost of wilderness training exceeds $1,000 per person, plus travel, lodging, and meal costs. The article indicated that over 4,000 people from Philip Morris alone have been sent to these programs in the past five years. Philip Morris managers must have enjoyed being out in the fresh, smoke-free air. With over $4,000,000 spent on these programs alone (not counting the lost time and the 4,000 weeks of lost productivity), Philip Morris could have done much better by training managers in methods more relevant to their responsibilities.

The same article casually reports that only two deaths have occurred among the 180,000 people who have attended the program. Two deaths and countless injuries are apparently no great sacrifice for a program that doesn't train managers to manage.

CEOs must look into these approaches very carefully. If mountain climbing and rope jumping are valid systems of training managers, how are they going to train managers who are not physically able to participate in the training? Are we going to say that a person with a bad back or who is in a wheel chair does not qualify to be a manager? Management training must include the unique skills and knowledge which are applicable to the level of managerial or supervisory position in question. Basic skills in human behavior should be considered as a personal development program, and not as management development skills.

There was an article in the Los Angeles Times in 1986 about Cypher Data and Mr. Gary Liebl, then CEO of

Cypher Data Products. Mr. Liebl had taken his management group to an Outward Bound expedition in order to train them to manage better in the "constantly changing environment in the computer industry." A full description of the training indicated, "Outward Bound's nine instructors led the managers through a course that forced participants to rely upon each other's strengths-both physical and mental-and to acknowledge their own weaknesses."

There were other experiences, such as blindfolding one member and locating him in the middle of an imaginary acid-filled pool with the " death" sentence upon him unless he could receive the cure within twenty minutes. The article quoted Mr. Liebl as saying, "the exercises such as the 'acid river' course stressed the importance of participative management."

Having read the article we decided to write to the Los Angeles Time's Business Editor. We wrote, "It is unfortunate that organizations in search of a panacea will try anything, no matter how irrelevant.... [we] find outrageous the concept that executives will create 'trust' among themselves by literally leading each other blindfolded. Chief Executives who look for blind trust among their executives are either naive or on an ego-trip... Time spent on clarifying organizational objectives and assigning unique accountabilities to each level of management will produce a better result than wandering blindfolded in the wilderness, 'trusting' another to lead them to safety."

To our surprise, Mr. Liebl read our comments and responded to us, starting a brief correspondence between Mr. Liebl and us. In his letter he mentioned that they had been "carefully clarifying organizational objectives." He also defended the Outward Bound experience as a learning experience which provided insights as to the nature of team dynamics. He concluded his letter by saying, "I do not necessarily expect...that the content of the letter will change your minds. If you would like to discuss this issue further, I would enjoy talking with you."

We wrote a two-page letter basically indicating that we have observed that many organizations follow the fads of the day. We believe that when the so-called learning experience is far removed from the basic realities of the organization, the result will be, at best, irrelevant if not damaging. Then we listed some of the "fads" that had come and gone by 1986: the human relations of the '50s, the Sensitivity Training of Carl Rogers, EST of the '60s, and Quality Circles of the '70s.

We ended the letter by saying that "if you can document pragmatic successes from these learning experiences, please send us as many crows as you can find and we will get busy eating them!"

Over the ensuing years we watched Cypher Data's progress with interest, as they were sold several times, and we wondered whether any of those who had gone through the acid-river exercise still worked for Cypher, and if they do, do they even remember what the experience was all about. If they remember it at all, it will more than likely be similar to recalling a party during which some unusual games were played. We seriously doubt if anyone will recall any insights into becoming better managers as a result of the experience.

While wilderness training and Seven Habits training may result from arbitrary decisions made by top management, many other instances of wasted training resources come through mismanagement, primarily involving the inability to integrate meaningful training into fundamental business practices. Digital Equipment Corporation (DEC) was a prime example.

Digital was a typical high-tech organization. The prevailing business motto was, "invent and sell." Everything else took a back seat. While Digital was making high profits on its inventions and was able to sell what they produced, there were no apparent problems for the management of DEC. Or were there? It seems that DEC always had management problem, but high profits and happy stockholders masked those problems. Their management philosophy was that managing is only for those people who deal with menial tasks such as production, receiving, and shipping. In Research and in Sales, managing was not a priority.

The only significant area of training was sales training which included a number of courses, primarily devoted to product knowledge. A large training staff in the corporate sales training department developed these courses which were mandatory for the sales staffs in all three regions of the country. The regional training groups, headed by a training manager, usually delivered these courses. Almost all of the courses were three days in length, regardless of the subject matter.

As soon as a product was conceived, the corporate sales training group would design a corresponding course. The course designers were a group of bright people who unfortunately had no idea what the line organization needed or wanted. When the sales slump hit Digital, the pressure on sales increased accordingly. Digital also decided to increase the number of products so they could fulfill their advertising motto, "We provide what you need." Of course, the product increase required more three-day sales training programs. However, the sales group had no time for training. They had to sell. The result was that the regional vice presidents were criticized for not holding enough sales training programs.

No matter how often line managers asked for less training time for each new product, the corporate sales training group refused, reasoning that if they reduced the training time, the attendees would not be able to demonstrate or describe the products effectively and sales would be lost.

Instead of solving the training versus sales problems, they added a new series of training sessions on teamwork. Their rationale was that more sessions would overcome the apparent lack of cooperation among the sales people and the line managers. At the same time that training was being conducted on teamwork, a management memo came down telling the sales people that if they didn't meet their personal sales quota, they would be dismissed. What happened to the teamwork concept? And why weren't Digital's top executives aware of these contradictions, these obstacles to performance?

If they couldn't see the problems, why didn't they listen to others who did and discuss the issues with them? When asked, their response in effect was, "Not to worry, we have finally found the problem-our people simply do not trust each other. If we can build trust in them, problems will be solved. That's why we have arranged for our managers to attend a class in Survival Training." Talk about throwing good money after bad.

Of course, the net result was that Digital stock took a drastic dive, as the company struggled through serious downsizing and product elimination. Unfortunately, Digital did not learn its lesson (as IBM did) and still couldn't connect their management problems with these makeshift training decisions. We predicted that as soon as they started to make money, the vicious cycle will start again simply because their management culture is not to manage. Fortunately, their merger with Compaq Computers has forced them to change their ways.

CEOs must realize that learning-and, more importantly, meaningful application of learning-does not come in quantum leaps. Learning is a process. In the practical aspects of behavior modification based on B.F. Skinner's work, a concept has been developed that is a good guide for CEOs. It is called "successive approximation." This concept tells us that people don't jump from one behavior to the next in quantum leaps. They begin by approximating that behavior, and then successively they come closer to the desired behavior.

This concept is true in nature, as it is true in organizations. Children do not simply stand up and run. They begin with the effort to stand up, then take the first step, then fall, and then get up and try again. Only then will children learn how to walk, let alone to run. Managers also do not fully develop or reach their full potential in the time it takes to complete a training program (especially when the program is an irrelevant one). Managers develop by performing desired skills daily on their job. Every successive attempt will make the managers better in the skill being practiced.

The organizations that have succeeded over the long haul are those that have resisted every fad-and-flavor-of-the-month-management-approach and refused to chase quick fix, imaginary solutions. Axiom: the best time to stay the course of fundamental management principles is all the time, especially during the good times.

In evaluating management fundamentals, don't concern yourself with how old the concepts are, but rather with how effective they are. Management fundamentals are not fashions that must be changed every year. Total Quality Management, which most organizations think is new, is one of the oldest ideas in management. All of it is based on the works of Allan Mogensen-in the year 1932. Of course neither Deming nor Juran ever credited Allan Mogensen for his Work Simplification Program which made an enormous contribution to the concept of effective management.

Trust Line Managers

The success of any organization depends on the strength of its line organization. Superiority of staff functions over line functions lasts only as long as the organization has a monopoly of products or services. (IBM was a good example.) What did the superiority of the staff function do to IBM? It took the company to the edge of disaster.

The line organization is the closest work unit to the customer and to the needs of the market. They, the line managers, must decide what to do. When the line organization doesn't have the right skills or the right approach to implement a decision, then staff can help. In short, ideally, when the line has decided what to do, the staff can consult with them on how best to do it.

Drucker recognized the line vs. staff problem in the early '50s. In his classical book on management, The Practice of Management, he wrote, "In every large company I know, the biggest organizational problem is the relationship between these service Staffs and the Managers they are supposed to serve. On paper the concept makes sense. But in practice it does not seem to work out. Instead of serving the manager, the service Staffs tend to become his master. Instead of deriving their objectives from the need and objectives of his business, they tend to push their own specialty as if it were an end in itself." Possibly these words are too harsh for current times, but his conclusion was true and remains true today.

All too often, staff personnel undermine the manager's responsibility instead of enabling the manager to do a better job. The smart CEO should adhere strictly to Drucker's admonition in this area, "Staff should have no authority over Operating Managers. It should never be allowed to hold power over promotions in Operating Management; for whoever controls a man's promotion controls the man. They (the Staff personnel) shouldn't work out policies, procedures, or programs for Operating Managers. These assignments are one of the major development opportunities within the business. To have them pre-empted by service professionals deprives a business of one of its most badly needs opportunities to develop managers."

We have seen that failure to heed the advice of one of the greatest management philosophers (Drucker) this century has caused enormous problems for organizations. By simply practicing the following management principle as described in Chapter 7, CEOs can begin to solve this long-lasting problem:

Hold all your Line Managers accountable for all

acts, activities, performances, behaviors, morale, etc., of all those people who report to them and only those people.

Such management practices ensure that all line managers make the internal management decisions. If there's a need for a program, a process, or a policy, the line managers should implement them. Simply stated, the line managers should ask for the staff's advice instead of having the staff tell the line managers what to do.

In a research program done for Motorola, Bob Galvin (then Motorola's CEO) became very interested in implementing various quality-related programs under the banner of Total Quality Management. As a result, a new series of programs were designed for all levels of managers, supervisors, team leaders, and mission workers. However, after a few years of conducting training, management felt that they were not getting the maximum results they wanted. They hired an outside consulting firm to find out why. After some research, the consultants discovered that only those units where senior managers reinforced the training back on the job (by questioning the attendees and asking them to start utilizing the new techniques learned) the result was excellent: $33 returned for every $1 of investment in training. And the cost included the cost of salaries and benefits while the participants attended the training. The result in the rest of the organization was either a complete waste of money or an occasional improvement, just enough to pay for the training.

The irony is that Motorola, even after discovering that the involvement of senior managers with the trainees was the main factor that the training paid off, didn't implement the approach in other areas of the company. The reason was that a staff unit discovered the results and wanted to take over the implementation of the process. Unfortunately, but perhaps predictably, the staff solution was to increase the number of programs.

No organization, no authority, can implement a program successfully unless it is done through the line management. The only way a CEO can implement a policy, a program, or a new culture successfully is by doing so with his or her management groups first and then by holding them accountable to implement it within their units.

The concept that the line needs come before the staff needs must be supported by the CEO daily. Otherwise, the organization will suffer the severe problems IBM, Digital Equipment, and GM had to deal with in the recent past.

THE CEO'S ROLE IN DOWNSIZING

The best approach to avoid downsizing is not to get too fat in the first place. Of course, legitimate problems can arise when an organization faces no option but to downsize. Lately, however, it has been fashionable to downsize even when there is no financial need.

Downsizing creates critical side effects: psychological and financial pressures on those who are asked to leave, and an aura of doubt and suspicion on those who remain. An organization is never the same and the employees are never as dedicated after a downsizing as they were before. It may take many years of stable operation before the employees will begin to get back to their previous enthusiasm.

Recently some organizations that were downsized recognized it, in hindsight, as a mistake. Bell Atlantic North through re-engineering and cost cutting programs lost as many as 14,000 line installers and clerical staff. Later the company found out that it needed most of them. Boeing Company decided that a downsized organization needed to be able to handle the flood of the orders through re-engineering. That did not work according to Boeing's plan. When orders started to pile up Boeing could not find enough people to hire to perform the job, and consequently because of delays took heavy losses. It is ironic that a company loses money because it has too many orders and the more orders it receives the more it loses.

Aetna Inc., after merging with U.S. Healthcare in 1996, cut five thousand staff members in its claims processing unit. One year later they found out that it was a mistake. It is important to quote Edward E. Lawler III, management professor at the University of Southern California, in his keen observation as reported to Aaron Bernstein (Business Week, June 8, 1998): "Most big firms have tried some version of re-engineering, but many got burned and won't do it again." Lawler also said: "These overhauls fail because they are 'top-down' ones orchestrated by consultants or executives not in operations. They demoralize the remaining workers and hurt productivity."

We support Lawler's observation completely and remind the readers of a statement we have made several times in this book. Very often changes occur in many organizations based on a book written by those who have not worked in a corporate structure, especially in the operating units. The theorists write books and present the "new" approach to management. CEOs who have not come up through an operating unit, who have no idea of the operation, become impressed with the "new" idea. Many of the current "new" approaches result in drastic downsizing. Often the board of directors rewards the CEO immediately for downsizing before any of the consequences are known.

An example of this phenomenon is what happened at Sunbeam with Al Dunlap. The Board approved a compensation package for Mr. Dunlap worth $70 million. Graef Crystal, a compensation consultant, maintained, "From this salary we know Al Dunlap is no risk taker. Secondly, he is careless with shareholder money, and so is his board."

Mr. Charles Elson, a Sunbeam director and a law professor at Stetson University, defends the board's decision by saying, "Look, it's not an inexpensive package; we know that. But on the other hand, it is a competitive labor market. There is clearly demand for his services at many other companies which would be willing to pay him a lot more." This is a very telling statement by a law professor (who must have had a great deal of operating experience). The board had bought Dunlap's self-evaluation. He proclaimed, "The best bargain is an expensive CEO." Mr. Dunlap has said publicly that he is worth every penny in his new contract. We are reminded of the famous saying: "a sucker is born every minute." We add to that saying that many of them must have become board members at Sunbeam.

Of course Mr. Dunlap's technique backfired this time. The same board that glorified his position and gave him a big employment contract fired him after a few weeks. It shows what happens to a board when they have a sizeable share of the company themselves. When the legal questions started to challenge the profit picture Mr. Dunlap had shown, the board decided it is time to ask this "genius" to peddle his techniques elsewhere.

Mr. Dunlap had said of his own talent, "Because some executives can't make decisions or constantly make the wrong ones, their incompetence virtually screams out for an Al Dunlap." We are wondering which executives, inept and incompetent or not, are going to hire him now?

Many people have maintained the concept that the organization cannot move to greatness by shrinking. But pseudo-CEOs such as Dunlap are not interested in the greatness of the organization. They are after self-enrichment. They never stay in a company that they've butchered long enough to suffer the consequences. They are proud of their style and maintain that they are saving the companies even when salvation is not called for. However, Dunlap may be right on one account when he says "If you need someone at whom to shoot poison arrows, look for my predecessors at any company I've turned around. They are your villains."

Tom Peters called Dunlap "one of biggest jerks I have ever met in my life." We feel Peters was too kind. Dunlap occupies a unique position; he is the worst of the Greed-Mongers and the Bean Counters combined. These types of CEOs don't need our advice and they won't change their behavior no matter how much sound input they receive. To them, "honor," "trust," "virtue," "unity," and "equilibrium" are all hollow words to laugh about on the way to the bank.

The middle managers that were cut at the rate of 23,000 per month in the early 1990s are in great demand now. Organizations have suddenly discovered that they lost some of their best and most experienced people, many to their competitors. They also discovered what happens when you lose your experienced employees you lose all of the collective knowledge they have accumulated. Who's left to do the important work, to solve the critical problems, and to transfer the necessary knowledge and expertise to the younger employees?

Downsizing creates insecurity among workers even when the jobless rate is very low. People do not want to change jobs. They change because they have to. In a survey appearing in USA Today (August 29, 1997) 70 percent of respondents say they have less job security than they did twenty or thirty years ago. Seventy-three percent say that there is more stress on the job now-caused by feeling of insecurity. These concerns are made at a time when media and the politicians are talking about the best economic time in decades. This is only further verification that statistics are not dependable and do not tell the whole story. The jobless rate is low because there are many workers who have two or three jobs in order to provide a living for their family.

CEOs facing possible downsizing should ask themselves:

1. Is there any possibility of handling the downsizing by natural attrition and in a reasonable time?

2. Can we give the people who will be affected some extra time, even as much as six months? Can

we change assignments to find out if we could increase our sales if everyone attempted to bring in more customers?

3. Can we experiment with optional ideas that we've never tried before for the next six months to find out if they work?

4. Can we find new markets for our services or products, using our own people's talents?

5. Can we all reduce our compensation by "x" percentage so that we don't have to lay off anyone?

6. Can we ask our people to work 10 to 20 percent less for 10 to 20 percent less pay?

When none of the above approaches is practical, then downsizing must take place. In downsizing, it is better to think carefully and announce all the anticipated changes at once rather than offer the news piecemeal.

Once downsizing takes place, the remaining employees must know that the downsizing is over and that everyone must get back to work. Hopefully, the company will be managed in such a way to avoid another downsizing.

With very few exceptions, neither downsizing nor re-engineering produces successful results. Downsizing that seemed to have worked show only short-term benefits- with little assurance that they will provide good results in the long term. In an article called "Breaking the Functional Mind-Set in Process Organizations," (Harvard Business Review, September-October, 1996) Ann Majchrzak and Qianwei Wang wrote, "Companies have endured the trauma of re-engineering only to discover that their performance is no better, and is in some cases actually worse, than before." They added, "Our research indicates that if companies are not ready to take the steps required to change their culture, they may be better off leaving their functional departments intact."

The question is why go through this downsizing trauma if performance is no better and is, in some cases, actually worse, than before? It is amazing that change, chaos, and trauma are the characteristics of New Age management while at times making organizational performance worse and producing poor results.

MANAGING WITHOUT THE CEO: SUMMARY STATEMENT

Top management and its role in external management brings our discussion full circle. We have emphasized the concepts of the hierarchy of knowledge and the levels of discontinuity, stressing that each level of management requires the development of a unique set of skills. It is also important to recognize that if each level does not attain these special skills, the levels below and above are severely hampered in carrying out their specialized functions

This is most important at the supervisory level. The mission work of any organization is so critical and costly that it will be supervised, hopefully by supervisors. However, if the supervisory level is weak or is diverted from full supervision, then managers will be pulled down to carry out this function, producing a void at the middle management level.

Any void created in the process may well be filled by adding layers of management or by forcing top management into playing an active internal management role. Who then will carry out top management's external functions? The answer is not "nobody." Your competition is eagerly waiting for the day when your top management is no longer visible in the marketplace, customer boardrooms, or in the halls of Congress.